# WordPress for Everyone

## Build Websites Without Coding

First English Edition

By

## Sameer Walke

# WordPress For Everyone

Build Websites Without Coding

Published by Sameer Walke

Registered Office: At Post Bembal, Ta. Mul, Dist. Chandrapur, Maharashtra, India 441228

Email: talktowalke@gmail.com

Phone/Whatsapp: +91-7499422093

Website: www.wordpressforeveryone.com

**Copyright © 2024 By Sameer Walke**

*ISBN 978-93-340-4965-7*

All rights reserved. No part of this book may be reproduced, stored in a retrieval system, or transmitted in any form or by any means, electronic, mechanical, photocopying, recording, or otherwise, without the prior written permission of the publisher.

***

To Sugandh Khobragade, for introducing WordPress to me.

# Content



***

# Introduction

This book began its journey as a set of notes created to teach my Marathi and Hindi students the fundamentals of WordPress. The positive response and continuous suggestions from my students encouraged me to transform these notes into a comprehensive guide. While working on the Marathi and Hindi versions, several associates recognized the potential for a wider reach and urged me to create an English version as well. This is how "WordPress for Everyone" was born, aiming to help you become a WordPress developer without coding.

## What is WordPress?

For starters, WordPress is software that allows you to build and manage websites without any coding knowledge. This type of software is called a Content Management System (CMS), and WordPress is the most popular CMS in the world.

WordPress is a free and open-source platform, meaning it's readily available for anyone to use. It offers easy-to-use tools, including drag-and-drop functionality, that allow you to build websites visually without needing to code. Nearly half of all websites on the internet are built on WordPress, showcasing its popularity and versatility.

## Who is this book for?

This book is for anyone who wants to learn how to build a website with WordPress, regardless of their technical experience. It is especially helpful for:

- **Beginners with no prior experience in website development**. This book will guide you step-by-step through the process of creating a website with WordPress, from choosing a hosting provider and domain name to installing WordPress, customizing your website, and creating different types of content.

- **People who want to learn how to build a website without coding.** This book focuses on using WordPress's visual editor and drag-and-drop tools, so you don't need to know any coding to create a beautiful and functional website.

- **Small business owners** who want to build their own website to promote their business and attract new customers.

- **Bloggers** who want to start a new blog or improve their existing blog.

- **Artists and creatives** who want to showcase their work online and build a following.

- **Ecommerce entrepreneurs** who want to build an online store and sell products or services.

This book covers the basics of WordPress and provides you with the knowledge and confidence to build a website that meets your needs, regardless of your technical background.

# What you will learn in this book

This book is designed to provide you with all the essential information you need to get started as a WordPress developer, in a concise and easy-to-reference format.

In **Part 1, "Getting Started with WordPress,"** you will learn what WordPress is and why it's a great choice for building your website. You will also learn how to choose a hosting provider and domain name, install WordPress, navigate the WordPress dashboard, and choose and install themes and plugins.

**Part 2, "Building Your Website,"** will teach you how to create and edit pages and posts, including formatting text, adding images and media, and using other content creation tools. You will also learn how to optimize images for web use, add navigation and menus to your website, and customize your website with widgets.

**Part 3**, "**Creating Different Types of Websites**," will show you how to build a variety of websites using WordPress, including blogs, business websites, e-commerce websites, social media websites, and LMS websites. You will learn about the specific features and functionalities needed for each type of website and how to implement them using WordPress tools and plugins.

Finally, **Part 4**, "**Resources and Next Steps**," will provide you with tips on troubleshooting common WordPress issues, a curated list of useful resources and further learning opportunities, and a glossary of key WordPress terms for easy reference.

My goal is to empower you to build a website that meets your needs, regardless of your technical background, and to provide you with a solid foundation for your journey as a WordPress developer.

***

# Acknowledgment

First and foremost, I extend my deepest gratitude to my best friend, Sugandh Khobragade, who was my first teacher into the world of WordPress. I am also eternally grateful to my family—my sister, father, and grandmother—for their unwavering support throughout my journey.

I wish to express my sincere thanks to my friends Akshay Bambode, Vijay Nilamwar, Arnab Mondal, Pranay Raut, Deepak Arya, Gaurav Kadwe, Sankalp Gurumukhi, Nikhil Ramteke, Manoj Wankhede, Kundan Wakde, Rakesh Bawne, Pritam Khobragade, Sumit Bambode, Swapnil Maraskolhe, Tushar Derkar, Tejas Mahadole, Shailesh Kankalwar, Nishtha Sawhney, Nitisha Tumble, Prajakta Tatkondawar, Nimisha Tiwari, Rucha Warhekar and Nibedita Sahu. Their invaluable insights and assistance have been instrumental in my development as a professional.

I am deeply indebted to my professional mentors, Pradeep Shukla (Dubai), Arun (Bengaluru), Demien (Nairobi), Senthil Kumar (Chennai/Dubai), Basundhara (Kolkata) and Jasmine Kaur (Toronto), for their trust and the opportunities they provided me. Their guidance has helped me navigate challenges and avoid pitfalls. This book would not have been possible without their belief in my abilities.

My heartfelt thanks go out to all my colleagues at SS Marketing, including Siddhant Walke, Nirant Urade, Sandesh Wakde, Rushikesh Nimgade, Yash Nandigramwar, Prajwal Timade, Sahas Wakde, Nishkarsh Nimgade,  Sudhan Khobragade, Ayush Wankar, Ajay Nilamwar, Shailesh Gaddekar, Lakshmikant Mandade, Prem Dharne, Tejas Kove,  Samit Gowardhan, Pranay Bolliwar, Rahul Guntikwar and Rohit Khobragade. Their constant support and presence have been invaluable.

Finally, I extend a heartfelt thank you to everyone reading this book and engaging with my online content, including those who follow me on Facebook, LinkedIn, and other social media platforms. Your interaction, support, and contributions enrich the online world and make it a truly meaningful space.

***

# Part 1

# Getting Started with WordPress

# Chapter 1: Understanding WordPress - A Simple Explanation

What will you learn:



## 1.1 What is WordPress?

*Fig. 1.1 Worpress.org home page*

**WordPress is a tool for building websites**. It's a content management system (CMS) that makes creating and managing your website content easy, even if you don't know how to code.

Think of it like this: **WordPress provides the building blocks and tools, and you get to design and assemble your website** just the way you want it.

This book focuses on the self-hosted version of WordPress (WordPress.org) (Fig .1.1), which gives you the most control and flexibility over your website.

Millions of people around the world use WordPress to power their websites, from simple blogs to complex online stores.

## 1.2 Brief History of WordPress

WordPress has come a long way since its humble beginnings in 2003. Initially conceived as a simple blogging platform, it has evolved into a powerful and versatile content management system (CMS) capable of powering diverse websites.

The story begins with **Matt Mullenweg** and **Mike Little** (Fig 1.2), who envisioned a user-friendly platform for anyone to share their thoughts and ideas online. **Building upon the existing b2/cafelog software, they created WordPress**, emphasizing ease of use and open-source development.

*Fig. 1.2 Matt Mullenweg (left) & Mike Little (right)*

Over the years, WordPress has undergone significant transformations, marked by major updates that introduced new features and functionalities. Some notable milestones include:

**Humble Beginnings (2003):**

- WordPress emerged as a fork of b2/cafelog, a blogging platform.

- Matt Mullenweg and Mike Little led the development, focusing on user-friendliness and flexibility.

**Early Growth (2004-2008):**

- WordPress gained traction due to its ease of use and open-source nature.

- The plugin and theme ecosystem started flourishing, allowing users to customize their websites.

- Major releases like WordPress 2.0 (introducing a new admin interface) and 2.7 (adding features like automatic upgrades and built-in plugin installation) fueled further adoption.

**Maturity and Expansion (2009-Present):**

- WordPress evolved beyond blogging to become a full-fledged content management system (CMS).

- Features like custom post types, taxonomies, and the REST API expanded its capabilities.

- The community grew exponentially, with developers, designers, and users contributing to its success.

- Today, **WordPress powers over 40% of all websites on the internet**, from personal blogs to complex e-commerce sites.

**Key Factors in WordPress' Success:**

- **Open-source nature:** This allows anyone to contribute to its development and use it freely.

- **User-friendliness:** WordPress requires no coding knowledge, making it accessible to a wide audience.

- **Flexibility:** The plugin and theme system allows for endless customization possibilities.

- **Strong community:** A dedicated community of developers and users constantly improve and support WordPress.

WordPress's journey is a testament to the power of open-source software and a passionate community. It has democratized web publishing, allowing anyone to build a website regardless of technical expertise. As

WordPress continues to evolve, it remains a powerful and accessible platform for creating any type of website imaginable.

## 1.3 Key Concepts

Before diving into the world of WordPress, it's helpful to understand some key concepts that underpin the platform. These concepts will be referenced throughout the book and are essential for building and managing your website effectively.

**1. Content Management System (CMS):** WordPress is a CMS, which means it allows you to create, manage, and publish content on your website without needing to code. You can easily add text, images, videos, and other media to your site through a user-friendly interface.

**2. Posts and Pages:** These are the two main content types in WordPress:

- **Posts:** Typically used for timely content like blog articles, news updates, or announcements. Posts are displayed in reverse chronological order and can be categorized and tagged.

- **Pages:** Used for static content like your About page, Contact page, or product descriptions. Pages are generally timeless and don't follow a chronological order.

**3. Themes:** Themes control the visual appearance of your website. You can choose from thousands of free and premium themes, each offering different layouts, colors, fonts, and functionalities.

**4. Plugins:** Plugins extend the functionality of your website by adding specific features. There are plugins for almost everything, from SEO optimization and social media integration to e-commerce and contact forms.

**5. Widgets:** Widgets are small modules that can be added to designated areas of your website, such as the sidebar or footer. They provide additional functionality like displaying recent posts, social media feeds, or search bars.

**6. Media Library:** This is where you upload and manage all your media files, including images, videos, and documents. You can easily insert these media files into your posts and pages.

**7. Users and Roles:** WordPress allows you to create user accounts with different roles and permissions. This helps control who can access and modify your website.

**8. Dashboard:** The WordPress Dashboard is your website's control center. Here, you can manage content, customize your site, install themes and plugins, and access various settings.

Understanding these key concepts will provide a solid foundation for your WordPress journey. As you become more familiar with the platform, you'll be able to leverage these concepts to build and manage your website with confidence.

# 1.4 Why Choose WordPress?

With so many website building platforms available, you might be wondering why WordPress stands out as the top choice. Here are some compelling reasons why WordPress is the ideal platform for building your website:

**1. User-Friendly:** WordPress requires no coding knowledge, making it accessible to anyone. The intuitive interface allows you to easily create and manage content, customize your site, and install themes and plugins.

**2. Open-Source and Free:** WordPress is open-source software, meaning it's free to use and modify. This gives you complete control over your website and allows you to access the source code for further customization.

**3. Vast Community and Support:** WordPress boasts a massive and active community of developers, designers, and users. This translates to extensive resources, tutorials, forums, and support available online, ensuring you can always find help when needed.

**4. Flexibility and Scalability:** WordPress can power any type of website, from simple blogs to complex e-commerce stores and membership sites. Its flexibility allows you to customize your site to meet your specific needs, and it can grow with your business as your requirements evolve.

**5. Extensive Theme and Plugin Ecosystem:** One of WordPress's biggest strengths is its vast library of themes and plugins. You can choose from thousands of free and premium options to customize your website's appearance and functionality without needing to code.

**6. SEO-Friendly:** WordPress is built with search engine optimization (SEO) in mind. Its clean code and structure make it easy for search engines to crawl and index your website, improving your chances of ranking higher in search results.

**7. Secure and Reliable:** WordPress is constantly updated with security patches and improvements, ensuring your website remains secure and protected. Additionally, its large community of developers constantly scrutinizes the platform, identifying and fixing vulnerabilities quickly.

**8. Cost-Effective:** While WordPress itself is free, you may need to invest in web hosting, domain registration, and potentially premium themes or plugins. However, compared to other website building platforms, WordPress offers a cost-effective solution with greater flexibility and control.

In conclusion, WordPress offers an unbeatable combination of user-friendliness, flexibility, affordability, and a supportive community. Whether you're a beginner building your first website or an experienced developer looking for a powerful platform, WordPress is an excellent choice.

# 1.5 Conclusion

WordPress has revolutionized web publishing, empowering individuals and businesses to build websites without technical limitations. Its user-friendly interface, vast customization options, and thriving community make it the platform of choice for millions across the globe.

In this chapter, we've explored the fundamentals of WordPress, from its origins and key concepts to the compelling reasons why it stands out as the leading website building platform. As you delve deeper into this book, you'll gain the knowledge and skills to harness the full potential of WordPress and create a website that meets your unique needs and aspirations.

Whether you're a blogger sharing your passion, a business owner establishing your online presence, or an artist showcasing your work, WordPress provides the tools and freedom to bring your vision to life. So, embark on this exciting journey and discover the endless possibilities that await you in the world of WordPress.

***

# Chapter 2: Choosing a Hosting Provider and Domain Name

What will you learn:



## 2.1 Introduction

Choosing the right hosting provider and domain name is akin to laying a solid foundation for your house. These two elements are crucial for your website's stability, performance, and success. While it might be tempting to rush through this step, taking the time to understand and choose wisely will pay dividends in the long run.

### What is a Domain Name?

Simply put, your domain name is your website's address on the internet. It's what people type into their browser to access your site. For example, "google.com" or "wordpress.org" are domain names (Fig 2.1). A good domain name should be memorable, relevant to your website's content, and reflect your brand identity.

### What is Web Hosting?

Web hosting is the service that stores your website's files and makes them accessible to visitors online. Think of it as renting space on a server where your website resides. Different types of hosting offer varying levels of resources, performance, and support.

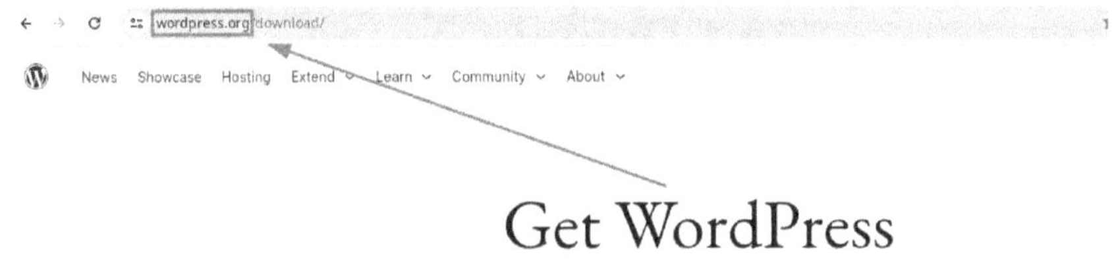


*Fig. 2.1 Domain name*

## Why Choosing the Right Domain and Hosting Matters?

- **Performance and Speed:** Your hosting provider significantly impacts your website's loading speed, which affects user experience and SEO ranking. A reliable hosting provider ensures your website runs smoothly and loads quickly for visitors.

- **Reliability and Uptime:** You want your website to be accessible to visitors at all times. Choosing a hosting provider with high uptime guarantees minimal downtime and ensures your website is always available.

- **Security:** A good hosting provider implements robust security measures to protect your website from cyberattacks and data breaches. This is crucial for safeguarding your website and your visitors' information.

- **SEO and Branding:** A well-chosen domain name can contribute to your SEO efforts and brand recognition. A memorable and relevant domain name is easier for users to remember and find, positively impacting your search engine ranking and brand identity.

Choosing the right domain name and hosting provider is an investment in your website's success. By understanding their importance and carefully evaluating your options, you'll lay a strong foundation for a website that performs well, attracts visitors, and reflects your brand effectively.

# 2.2 Understanding Web Hosting

Web hosting is the service that stores your website's files (code, images, videos, etc.) and makes them accessible to visitors online. Essentially, it's like renting space on a powerful computer (server) that's connected to the internet 24/7. When someone types your domain name into their browser, their computer connects to your web hosting server, which then delivers the website files to their screen.

## Types of web hosting

There are different types of web hosting available, each offering varying levels of resources, performance, and support:

**1. Shared Hosting:** This is the most common and affordable option, where multiple websites share resources on a single server. It's like living in a shared apartment building – you share resources like the kitchen and laundry room with other tenants. Shared hosting is suitable for small websites with low traffic, but it can be slower and less reliable than other options.

**2. Virtual Private Server (VPS) Hosting:** A VPS offers a dedicated portion of a server's resources, providing more control and better performance than shared hosting. It's like having your own apartment within a larger building – you have your own dedicated space and resources, but you still share the building with others. VPS hosting is ideal for websites with moderate traffic or requiring more customization and control.

**3. Dedicated Hosting:** With dedicated hosting, you rent an entire server exclusively for your website. This gives you the highest level of control, performance, and security, but it's also the most expensive option. It's like renting out an entire house – you have all the space and resources to yourself. Dedicated hosting is best suited for large websites with high traffic or demanding applications.

**4. Managed WordPress Hosting:** This type of hosting is specifically optimized for WordPress websites. It typically includes features like automatic WordPress updates, enhanced security, and specialized support from WordPress experts. Managed WordPress hosting can be a good choice for beginners who want a hassle-free experience and prioritize performance and security.

## Factors to Consider When Choosing a Hosting Provider

- **Price:** Hosting costs can vary significantly. While budget is important, prioritize reliability and performance over the cheapest option.

- **Storage Space and Bandwidth:** Consider your website's size and expected traffic to determine the necessary storage space and bandwidth.

- **Uptime:** Look for a hosting provider with a high uptime guarantee (ideally 99.9% or higher) to ensure your website is consistently accessible.

- **Customer Support:** Choose a provider with responsive and knowledgeable customer support to help you with any technical issues.

- **Security Features:** Ensure the hosting provider offers security features like firewalls, malware scanning, and regular backups.

- **Server Location:** Consider choosing a server located in your target audience's region for faster website loading times.

Choosing the right web hosting is crucial for your website's success. By understanding the different types of hosting and considering the essential factors, you can select a provider that meets your website's needs and budget.

# 2.3 Choosing a Domain Name

Your domain name is your website's unique address on the internet, like "google.com" or "yourwebsite.com." It's what people type into their browser to access your site, making it a crucial element of your online presence. Choosing the right domain name requires careful consideration, as it impacts your branding, SEO, and memorability.

## Tips for Choosing a Domain Name

- **Keep it short and memorable**: Aim for a domain name that's easy to remember and type. Avoid lengthy names or complex words that users might misspell.

- **Make it relevant to your website:** Your domain name should reflect your website's content and purpose. This helps users understand what your website is about and improves search engine optimization (SEO).

- **Use keywords strategically:** Including relevant keywords in your domain name can boost your SEO ranking. However, avoid keyword stuffing, as it can appear spammy.

- **Brand it:** If you have an established brand, incorporating your brand name into your domain name strengthens brand recognition and consistency.

- **Consider different domain extensions:** The most common domain extension is ".com," but other options like ".net," ".org," or niche-specific extensions like ".shop" or ".blog" are available. Choose an extension that aligns with your website's purpose and target audience.

- **Check for availability and trademark issues:** Before settling on a domain name, ensure it's available for registration and doesn't infringe on any existing trademarks.

## Domain Name Registration

Once you've chosen your ideal domain name, you need to register it through a domain registrar. Popular registrars include Hostinger, GoDaddy, Namecheap, and Google Domains. The registration process is typically straightforward and involves paying an annual fee.

**Remember:** Your domain name is a long-term investment in your online identity. Take your time, brainstorm creatively, and choose a domain name that is memorable, relevant, and reflects your brand effectively.

# 2.4 Connecting Your Domain and Hosting

After securing your domain name and choosing a hosting provider, the next step is connecting the two. This ensures that when someone types your domain name into their browser, they are directed to your website files stored on your hosting server.

The process of connecting your domain and hosting can vary slightly depending on your domain registrar and hosting provider. However, the general steps are as follows:

## 1. Obtain your Nameservers

Log in to your hosting account and locate your nameservers. These are typically two or more addresses that look like "ns1.yourhostingprovider.com" and "ns2.yourhostingprovider.com." Nameservers act like a directory, telling the internet where to find your website files.

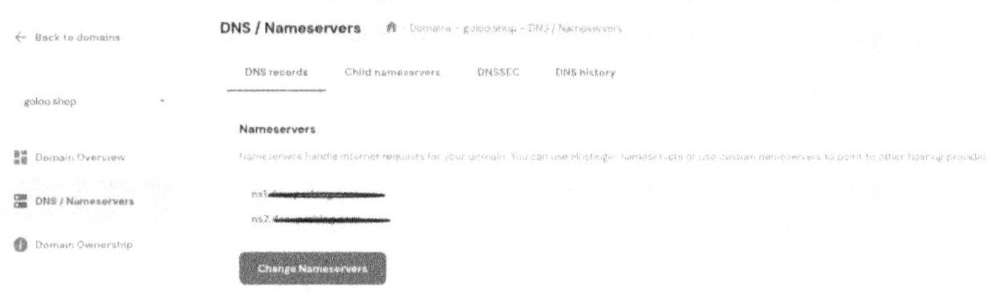

*Fig. 2.2  Changing nameservers of your domain*

## 2. Update your Domain's DNS settings

Log in to your domain registrar's control panel and find the DNS settings for your domain. You'll need to replace the existing nameservers (Fig. 2.2) with the ones provided by your hosting provider. This update tells the internet to look for your website files on your hosting server.

## 3. Propagation

After updating your DNS settings, it can take some time (usually 24-48 hours) for the changes to propagate throughout the internet. This means it may take a while before your website is accessible through your domain name.

## 4. Troubleshooting (Optional)

If you encounter any issues during the connection process, don't hesitate to contact your hosting provider or domain registrar for assistance. They can help you troubleshoot any problems and ensure your domain and hosting are correctly linked.

## Additional Notes

Some hosting providers offer domain registration services as well. If you register your domain name through your hosting provider, the connection process might be automatic or simplified.

It's important to keep your domain name and hosting account information secure and up-to-date. This helps prevent unauthorized access and ensures your website remains accessible to visitors.

By following these steps and troubleshooting any potential issues, you'll successfully connect your domain name to your hosting account, paving the way for your website to be accessible to the world.

# 2.5 Free Domain and Hosting Providers

Since you might be starting out and limited on upfront investment, there are free options available for obtaining a domain and hosting. However, it's important to note that free plans are generally not recommended for live projects due to limitations. For optimal performance, I recommend transitioning to a paid plan later on.

## Free Web Hosting Providers

Free web hosting services can be a great way to get your website up and running without spending any money. However, it's important to be aware of the limitations of free plans before you sign up. Here's a breakdown of what you can expect from free web hosting providers:

- **Limited resources:** Free plans typically come with limited storage space, bandwidth, and processing power. This means your website may be slow to load and may not be able to handle a lot of traffic.

- **No control panel:** Some free hosts don't provide a control panel, which makes it more difficult to manage your website.

- **Ads on your website:** Many free hosts display ads on your website, which can generate revenue for them but may not be ideal for your brand.

- **Uptime:** Free hosting providers may not offer the same level of uptime guarantees as paid providers. This means your website may be unavailable from time to time.

Here are some popular free web hosting providers to consider:

- InfinityFree
- GoogieHost
- Freehostia
- FreeHosting
- Hostinger (offers a free tier with limited features)

## Free Domain Providers

While it's less common, there are a few providers that offer free domain names. However, there are usually some restrictions associated with these offers, such as:

- **Subdomains:** Free domains are often subdomains of the provider's domain. This may not be ideal for branding purposes.

- **Limited availability:** Free domains may only be available for certain top-level domains (TLDs), such as .tk or .ml.

- **Renewal fees:** While the initial registration may be free, you may need to pay a renewal fee to keep your domain name after the first year.

Here are some things to keep in mind before you choose a free domain provider:

- **Read the terms and conditions carefully:** Make sure you understand the limitations and renewal fees associated with the free domain.

- **Consider a paid domain:** If you're serious about your website, it's often worth investing in a paid domain name from a reputable registrar. This will give you more control over your domain and a more professional look.

Here are some free domain providers to consider:

- **Freenom:** It is one of the most popular providers of free domains. They offer a variety of top-level domains (TLDs), such as .tk, .ml, .ga, .cf, and .gq. Keep in mind that these are not the most common TLDs, and may not be ideal for branding purposes.

- **Dot.TK:** It is another provider that offers free domains with the .tk TLD. Like Freenom, this TLD is not the most popular and may not be the best choice for branding.

Even though free domain providers exist, I generally recommend going with a paid domain registrar for better control, branding, and professionalism.

## 2.6 Conclusion

Choosing the right hosting provider and domain name are foundational steps in building a successful website. These decisions impact your website's performance, reliability, security, and branding. By taking the time to understand your needs and carefully evaluate your options, you'll set your website up for success.

Remember, your domain name is your digital address and your hosting provider is the foundation on which your website stands. Invest in reliable, secure, and high-performance solutions to ensure your website runs smoothly, attracts visitors, and reflects your brand effectively.

With a solid foundation in place, you can confidently move forward with building and customizing your WordPress website, knowing that it has a reliable and secure home on the internet.

***

# Chapter 3: Installing WordPress

What will you learn:



## 3.1 Introduction

Welcome to the exciting stage where your website starts to come to life! Installing WordPress is the crucial step that transforms your domain and hosting into a functional website. This chapter will guide you through the process of installing WordPress on two main environments: a web hosting server and a local server.

### Web Hosting Server

Installing WordPress on a web hosting server is the most common approach. This makes your website live and accessible to visitors on the internet. Most hosting providers offer user-friendly tools and one-click installation options, making this process relatively straightforward.

### Local Server

A local server is a simulated web server environment on your own computer. Installing WordPress locally allows you to develop and test your website without affecting your live site. This is a great option for experimenting with themes, plugins, and customizations before making them public.

### Which Method is Right for You?

The best installation method depends on your needs and technical comfort level. If you want to get your website up and running quickly and don't need extensive customization before launch, installing directly on your web hosting server is a good choice. However, if you prefer to experiment and develop your website in a safe, offline environment, installing WordPress on a local server might be a better fit.

This chapter will provide detailed instructions for both installation methods, allowing you to choose the approach that best suits your needs. Let's get started!

# 3.2 Installing WordPress on a Web Hosting Server

Installing WordPress on your web hosting server makes your website accessible to the world. This section will guide you through the process, covering both one-click installation and manual installation methods.

## One-Click Installation

Many hosting providers understand the popularity of WordPress and offer convenient one-click installation tools (Fig. 3.1). These tools automate the entire installation process, making it incredibly easy for beginners to get their WordPress website up and running quickly.

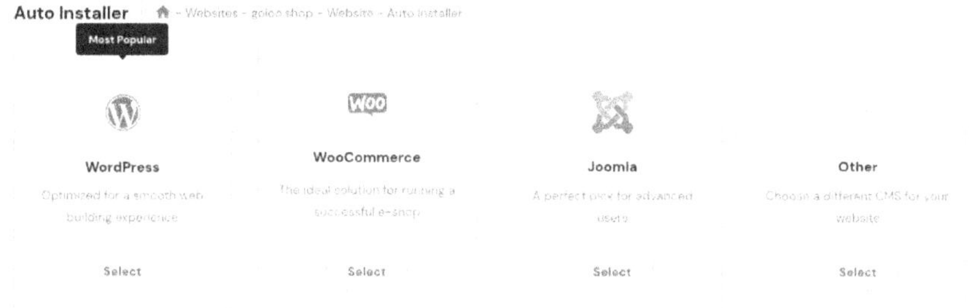


*Fig. 3.1 One-click Installation method*

Instead of manually downloading files, creating databases, and configuring settings, you can simply click a button (Fig. 3.2) and let the hosting provider handle everything behind the scenes. This eliminates the potential for errors and saves you valuable time.

Typically, you can find the one-click installation option within your hosting control panel. Look for a section dedicated to WordPress or website applications. Once you locate the WordPress installation tool, simply click on it and follow the on-screen instructions. You may need to provide some basic information like your desired website title and admin login details.

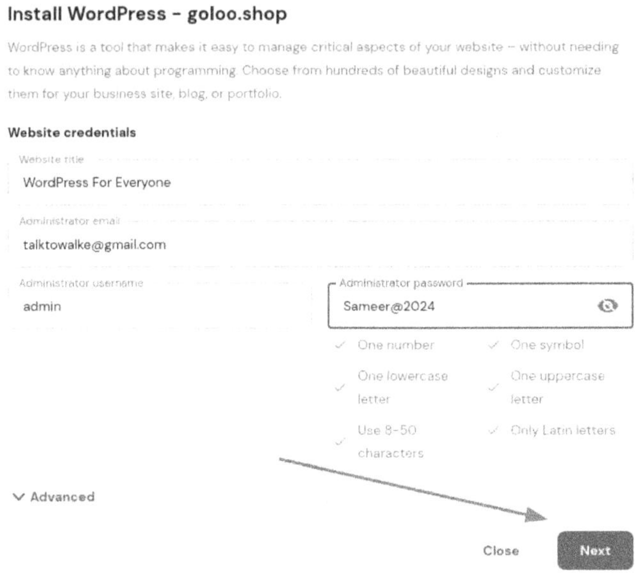


*Fig. 3.2 Creating website/admin credentials*

Within minutes, your WordPress website will be ready to go! This streamlined approach is ideal for beginners who want to avoid technical complexities and focus on building their website content and design.

## Manual Installation

If your web hosting provider doesn't offer a one-click installation for WordPress, you can still install it yourself. Here's a step-by-step guide:

1.  **Download WordPress:** Visit the official WordPress website (https://wordpress.org/download/) and download the latest version of the software as a zip file.

2.  **Create a Database:**

- Log in to your hosting control panel (cPanel or similar).

- Locate the section for managing databases (often labeled "Database" or "MySQL Database").

- Create a new database specifically for your WordPress website (Fig 3.3).

- Create a new user for this database and assign a strong password (Fig 3.3).

*Fig. 3.3 Creating database and user in Hostinger panel*

**Important:** Depending on your hosting provider, you might need to create the user separately and then grant them full privileges (ALL PRIVILEGES) for the newly created database (Fig 3.4).

Keep this information (database name, username, password) readily available, as you'll need it in the next step.

*Fig. 3.4 adding user to database*

3.  **Upload WordPress Files:** There are two common methods for uploading files to your hosting account:

- **FTP (File Transfer Protocol):** You'll need an FTP client software (like FileZilla) and your FTP login credentials (username and password) provided by your hosting provider.

- **File Manager (Recommended):** Most hosting providers offer a built-in file manager (Fig 3.5) within their control panel. This method is generally easier, especially for smaller uploads.

*Fig. 3.5 File Manager is the most common way to access your file.*

- Use whichever method you prefer to upload the downloaded WordPress zip file to the root directory of your website (often named "public_html").

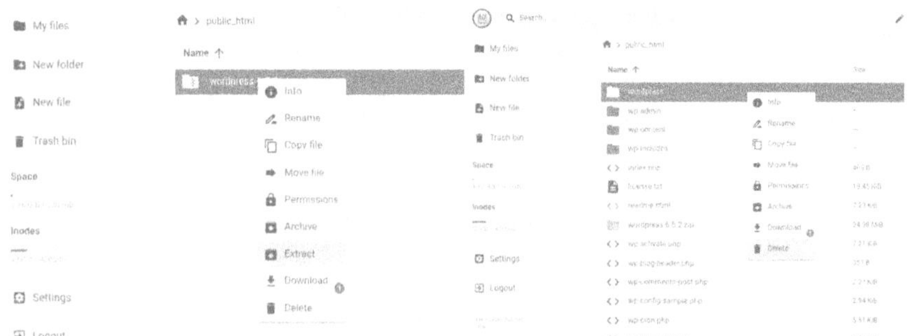

*Fig. 3.6 File manager easily lets you unzip WordPress files.*

- Unzip the file directly in the root directory. This might create a folder named "wordpress" containing all the extracted files. If this happens move all the extracted files out of the "wordpress" folder and into the root directory. And delete the empty "wordpress" folder.

- If you want to install WordPress in a subdirectory (e.g., domain.com/mydirectory/), upload and unzip the files directly within that subdirectory.

## 4. Run the Installation Script:

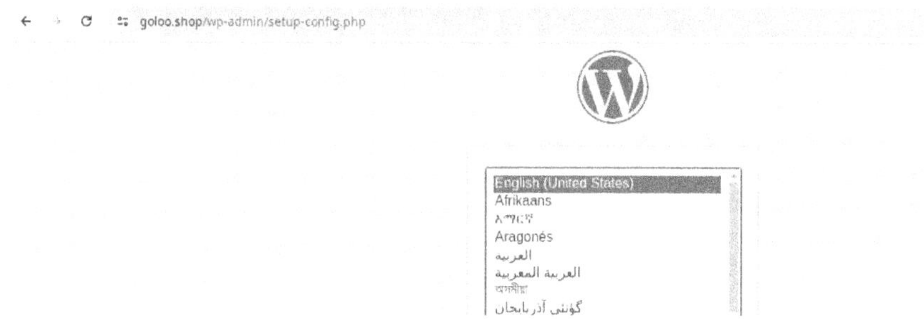


*Fig. 3.7 After entering a domain name, it will automatically redirect to begin the installation.*

- Open a web browser and navigate to your domain name (e.g., yourdomain.com for local server localhost/foldername). If you installed WordPress in a subdirectory, use the complete path (e.g., yourdomain.com/subdirectoryname).

- This will automatically launch the WordPress installation script (Fig 3.7).

- You'll be greeted with a welcome screen where you can choose your preferred language (Fig 3.7).

## 5. Connect to Database:

- The installation script will ask for your database information. Enter the details you gathered in step 2 (database name, username, and password) (Fig 3.8).

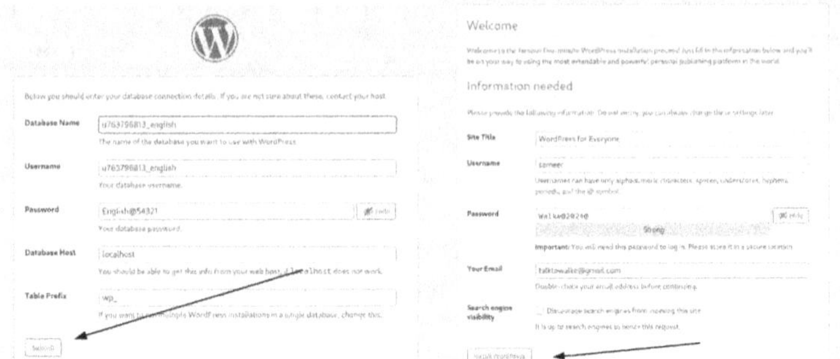

*Fig. 3.8 Connecting database and creating dashboard/admin user*

- Click "Submit" to establish the connection.

- If successful, you'll receive a confirmation message and an option to proceed with the installation.

## 6. Complete Installation:

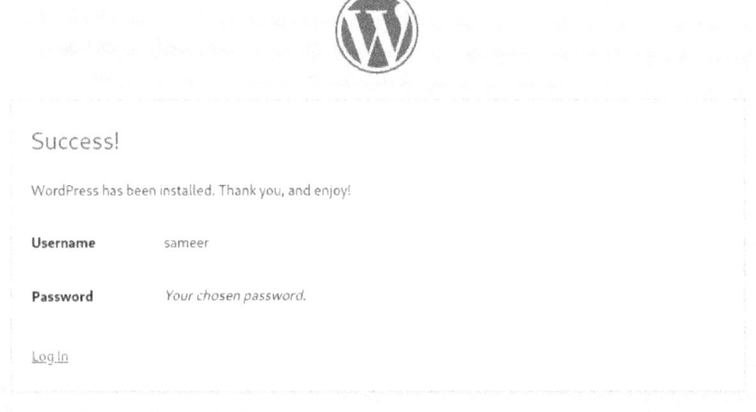


*Fig. 3.9 After successful installation, a 'success' message will appear.*

- Click on the "Run installation" button.

- Provide a title for your website and create a new administrative username (Fig 3.8) and password. This information will be used to log in to your WordPress dashboard later.

- Click "Submit" to initiate the installation process (Fig 3.8). WordPress will be installed automatically.

Once the installation is complete, you can log in to your WordPress dashboard using the username and password you created in step 6. This is where you'll manage your website content and settings.

## Troubleshooting

If you encounter any issues during installation, consult your hosting provider's documentation or contact their support team for assistance. Common issues include incorrect database information, file permission errors, or server configuration problems.

**Congratulations!** You've successfully installed WordPress on your web hosting server. Now you can log in to your WordPress dashboard and start building your website.

# 3.3 Installing WordPress on a Local Server

Installing WordPress on a local server creates a testing environment on your own computer, allowing you to develop and experiment with your website offline. This is a great way to familiarize yourself with WordPress, try out different themes and plugins, and test customizations without affecting your live website.

## Benefits of Local Development

- **Safe experimentation:** You can freely test changes and experiment with your website without worrying about breaking anything on your live site.

- **Offline access:** Work on your website even without an internet connection.

- **Faster development:** Local servers often run faster than live servers, allowing for quicker testing and development.

## Local Server Software

Several popular software options can create a local server environment on your computer. Some popular choices include:

- **XAMPP:** A free and open-source solution for Windows, macOS, and Linux.

- **MAMP:** A user-friendly option for macOS and Windows.

- **Local by Flywheel:** A powerful and user-friendly tool specifically designed for WordPress development.

- **WAMP**: Another free and open-source option for Windows users. It provides a user-friendly interface and easy setup for Apache, MySQL, and PHP.

These software options typically include all the necessary components to run a WordPress website locally, such as Apache web server, MySQL/MariaDB database, and PHP scripting language.

The best choice for you will depend on your operating system, technical preferences, and desired features. For example, Local by Flywheel offers a more streamlined and user-friendly experience specifically tailored for WordPress, while XAMPP and WAMP provide more flexibility and customization options.

## Installation Process

The specific installation process may vary depending on the local server software you choose. However, the general steps are as follows (please refer image from previous section):

1. **Install the local server software:** Download and install your chosen local server software, following the provided instructions.

2. **Create a database:** Use the local server software's tools to create a new database for your WordPress installation.

3. **Download WordPress:** Download the latest version of WordPress from https://wordpress.org/download/.

4. **Set up WordPress files:** Unzip the downloaded WordPress files

and place them in the designated directory within your local server environment. This directory or folder depends on the software you are using. Check the documentation of your local server provider.

5. **Run the installation script:** Open your web browser and navigate to the local server address (usually "localhost"). This will launch the WordPress installation script. Follow the on-screen instructions, providing the database information you created earlier. Now it same as like you installed in your web hosting.

6. **Set up your website:** Once the installation is complete, you can set up your website title, username, password, and email address.

## Testing and Troubleshooting

After installing WordPress locally, you can access your website in your web browser using the local server address. You can then test your website functionality, install themes and plugins, and experiment with customizations. If you encounter any issues, consult the documentation for your local server software or seek help from online forums and communities.

**Remember:** When you're ready to launch your website, you'll need to migrate it from your local server to your web hosting server. This process involves transferring your website files and database to your hosting environment.

Installing WordPress on a local server provides a safe and flexible environment for developing and testing your website. It's a valuable tool for both beginners and experienced WordPress users.

# 3.4 Post-Installation Steps

Congratulations! You've successfully installed WordPress, either on your web hosting server or locally. Now it's time to take some essential post-installation steps to transform your bare WordPress installation into a fully functional website.

## Logging in to WordPress

Access your WordPress dashboard by navigating to your website's domain name followed by "/wp-admin" (e.g., yourwebsite.com/wp-admin or localhost/foldername/wp-admin). Enter the username and password you created during installation to log in.

## Security Measures

Securing your WordPress website is crucial. Take these important security measures after installation:

- **Change the default login credentials:** Update the default username and password to strong and unique alternatives.

- **Update WordPress regularly:** WordPress releases regular updates that include security patches and bug fixes. Keep your WordPress installation, themes, and plugins updated for optimal security.

Remember: Building and customizing your WordPress website is an exciting journey that begins with these initial setup steps. In the next chapter, we'll delve deeper into the process of building your website, exploring how to create content, customize your design, and add powerful features using themes and plugins.

With the foundation laid in this chapter, you're now equipped to explore the vast world of WordPress and turn your website vision into reality.

# 3.5 Conclusion

Installing WordPress is the gateway to building your website, and choosing the right installation method depends on your individual needs and preferences.

If you prioritize speed and convenience, installing WordPress directly on your web hosting server using a one-click installation tool is a great option. However, if you value a safe and flexible environment for experimentation and development, installing WordPress on a local server might be a better fit.

***

# Chapter 4: Exploring the WordPress Dashboard

What will you learn:



## 4.1 Introduction

Congratulations on successfully installing WordPress! Now it's time to explore the heart of your website: the WordPress Dashboard. This is your central hub for managing and customizing every aspect of your website, from creating content and managing users to configuring settings and installing plugins.

Think of the Dashboard as your website's mission control. From here, you can monitor your website's performance, access essential tools, and make changes to your website's appearance and functionality. Whether you're a seasoned website developer or a complete beginner, the WordPress Dashboard is designed to be intuitive and user-friendly. It is also referred to as an **"admin panel"** or **"back-end"**.

This chapter will take you on a guided tour of the Dashboard, explaining its various sections, features, and functionalities. We'll explore how to manage your content, customize your website's appearance, install plugins, and configure settings. By the end of this chapter, you'll be comfortable navigating the Dashboard and confidently managing your WordPress website.

So, let's dive in and unlock the power of the WordPress Dashboard!

## 4.2 Dashboard Overview

The WordPress Dashboard is designed to be user-friendly and intuitive, even for beginners. Let's take a closer look at its layout and key features:

### Layout and Interface

- **Navigation Menu:** Located on the left-hand side (Fig 4.1), this menu provides access to all the essential WordPress functionalities, including posts, pages, media, comments, appearance, plugins, users, tools, and settings.

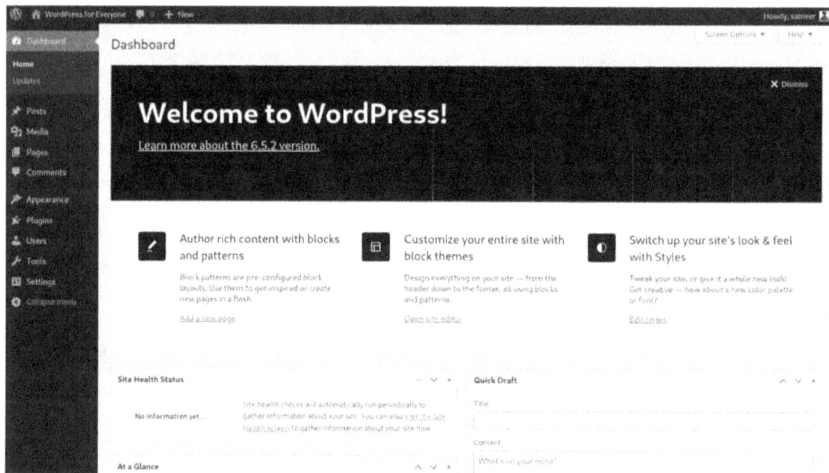

*Fig. 4.1 WordPress Dashboard home*

- **Toolbar:** Situated at the top of the screen (Fig 4.1), the toolbar offers quick access to frequently used functions like creating new posts or pages, managing comments, and accessing your profile.

- **Welcome Panel:** This panel, usually displayed at the top of the Dashboard (Fig 4.1), provides a welcome message, quick links to essential tasks, and an overview of your website's content and activity.

- **Additional Panels:** Depending on your installed plugins and themes, you may see additional panels on the Dashboard displaying relevant information and statistics.

## Screen Options and Help

Fig 4.2 Screen Options and Help

- **Screen Options:** Located at the top right corner of the Dashboard (Fig 4.2), this tab allows you to customize which panels are displayed on your Dashboard. You can show or hide specific panels based on your workflow and preferences.

- **Help:** The Help tab, also located at the top right corner (Fig 4.2), provides access to contextual help resources and documentation related to the specific section of the Dashboard you're currently viewing.

## Updates

Keeping your WordPress installation, themes, and plugins updated is crucial for security and performance. The Dashboard displays notifications when updates are available. You can easily update WordPress core, themes, and plugins directly from the Dashboard with a few clicks.

By familiarizing yourself with the Dashboard layout and its key features, you'll be well-equipped to navigate and manage your WordPress website effectively

# 4.3 Managing Content

The WordPress Dashboard provides a comprehensive set of tools for creating, editing, and organizing your website content. This section will explore the key features for content management:

## Posts and Pages

- **Posts:** Typically used for blog articles, news updates, or other time-sensitive content. Posts are displayed in reverse chronological order and can be categorized and tagged for organization.

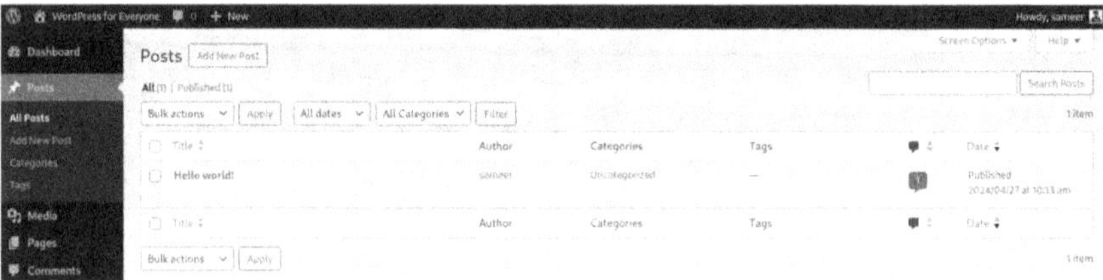

*Fig. 4.3 Posts*

- **Pages:** Used for static content like your About page, Contact page, or product descriptions. Pages are generally timeless and don't follow a chronological order.

*Fig. 4.4 Pages*

Both posts and pages are created and edited using the intuitive WordPress editor. You can add text, images, videos, and other media to your content, format it using various tools, and preview your changes before publishing.

## Categories and Tags

- **Categories:** Organize your posts into broad topics or subjects. For example, a food blog might have categories like "Recipes," "Restaurant Reviews," and "Cooking Tips."

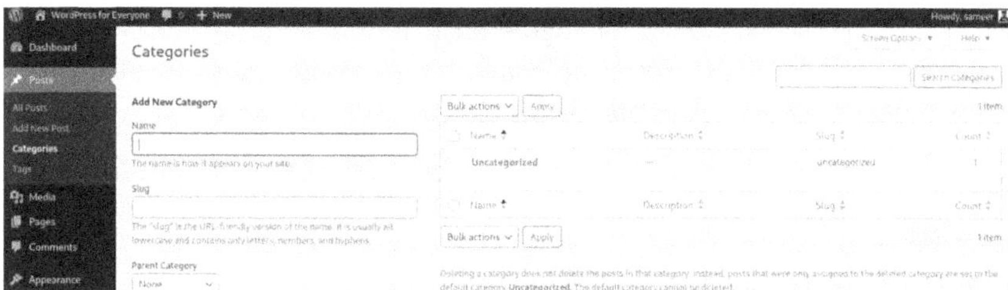

*Fig. 4.5 Categories*

- **Tags:** Assign specific keywords or terms to your posts to describe their content in more detail. For example, a recipe post might be tagged with "vegan," "dessert," and "chocolate."

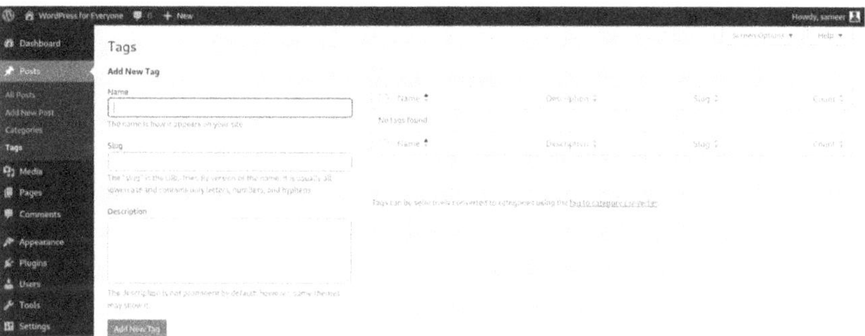

*Fig 4.6 Tags*

Categories and tags help users navigate your website and find relevant content. They also improve your website's search engine optimization (SEO) by providing additional information about your content.

## Media Library

The Media Library is your central repository for all your website's media files, including images, videos, documents, and audio files. You can upload new media files, manage existing ones, and easily insert them into your posts and pages.

## Comments

The Comments section allows you to moderate and manage comments left by visitors on your posts and pages. You can approve, reply to, edit, or delete comments, and configure comment settings to control spam and manage discussions on your website.

By mastering these content management features, you'll be able to create, organize, and publish engaging content that attracts and informs your website visitors

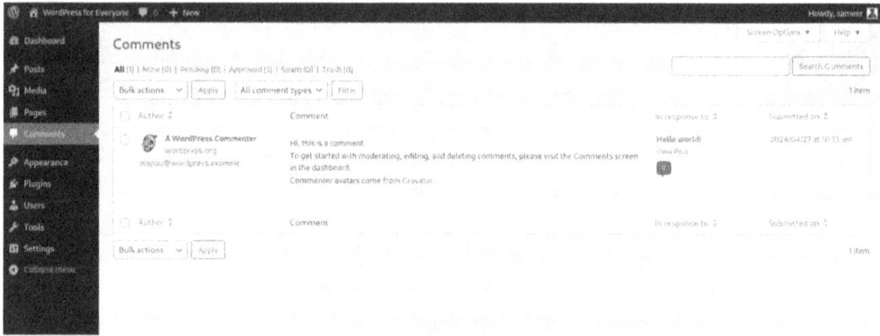

Fig. 4.7 Comments.

# 4.4 Appearance and Customization

The WordPress Dashboard offers a variety of tools to customize your website's appearance and create a unique and engaging experience for your visitors. This section will explore the key features for customizing your website:

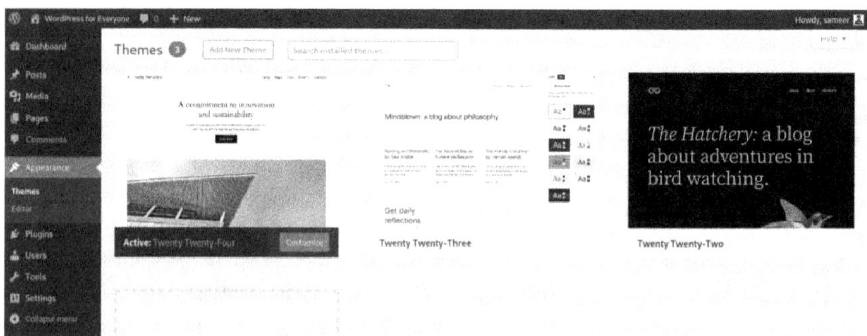

*Fig. 4.8 Appearance*

**Themes**

Themes control the overall design and layout of your website. WordPress

offers a vast library of free and premium themes, each with its own unique style and features. You can install and activate themes directly from the Dashboard, preview them to see how they look, and customize them further to match your brand and preferences.

When it comes to customizing the look and feel of your WordPress site, theme options play a crucial role. However, the way you access and utilize these options differs depending on whether you're using a classic theme (pre-WordPress 5.9) or a block theme (introduced in WordPress 5.9). Let's explore the options available in each category:

1.  **Classic Themes:**

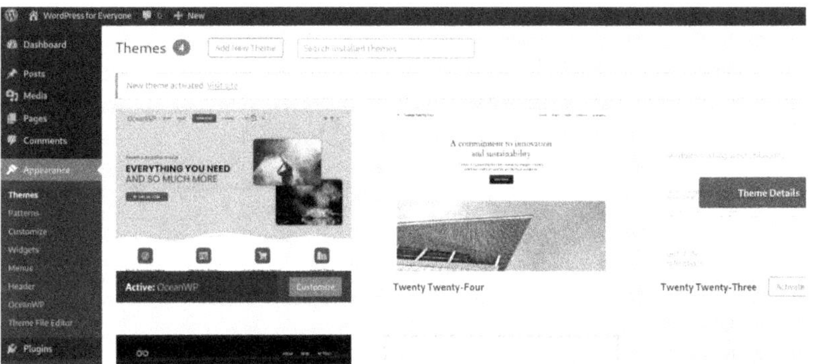

*Fig. 4.9 Appearance Section of OceanWP Theme*

- **Customize:** While some classic themes might offer limited live preview options here, it's not universally available. You might find basic controls for customizing colors, backgrounds, or header images.

- **Menus**: This section allows you to create, manage, and assign navigation menus to different areas of your website.

- **Widgets**: Widgets are interactive elements like calendars, social media feeds, or search bars that you can add to your sidebar or footer. You'll find a dedicated "Widgets" section where you can drag and drop widgets into designated widget areas.

- **Settings --> Reading**: This section controls how your blog posts are displayed. You can choose to show full posts or summaries on your homepage, set the number of posts displayed per page, and configure options for displaying comments.

- **Theme Options Panels**: Depending on the theme you're using, there might be additional options panels tucked under the "Appearance" section. These panels could be for customizing headers, footers, colors, typography, layouts, social media integration, and more. The specific options and their organization will vary based on the theme developer.

2. **Block Themes (Since 2023):** Block themes (WordPress 5.9+) offer a streamlined approach to website design. Let's explore the key areas within Appearance > Editor:

*Fig. 4.10 Editor Section of Twenty Twenty Four Theme*

- **Navigation:** Manage menus, just like classic themes.

- **Styles:** Control fonts, colors, and overall website aesthetics.

- **Templates:** The heart of block themes. Here, you get a live preview and can directly manipulate the layout using blocks (headers, footers, content areas, etc.).

- **Patterns:** Discover pre-designed block collections for faster website creation.

- **Settings > Reading:** Control blog post display (full posts/summaries, number of posts per page).

**Important Note:** Since block themes are a new approach, the location and availability of specific options might vary depending on the theme itself. Some block themes might offer dedicated theme options panels within the "Appearance" section, similar to classic themes. However, the focus with block themes is on using the block editor and the "Customize" section for most customizations.

By understanding these options and their locations, you can effectively personalize your WordPress website, whether you're using a classic theme or embracing the new world of block themes. Remember to explore the specific options offered by your chosen theme for a more complete picture of its customization capabilities.

# 4.5 Plugins and Functionality

Plugins are the building blocks that add specific features and functionalities to your WordPress website. They can enhance your website's SEO, improve security, add social media integration, create contact forms, and much more. The WordPress plugin directory offers a vast library of free plugins, and premium plugins with advanced features are also available from third-party vendors. We will be learning more about plugins in future chapters.

# 4.6 Users and Roles

WordPress allows you to create multiple user accounts with different roles and permissions. This is particularly useful for websites with multiple contributors or when you need to grant varying levels of access to different individuals.

## User Management

The "Users" section in the WordPress Dashboard allows you to:

- **Add New Users:** Create new user accounts by providing a username, email address, and password. You can also assign a specific role to the user.

- **Edit Existing Users:** Modify user information, including their password, email address, and role.

- **Delete Users:** Remove user accounts from your website.

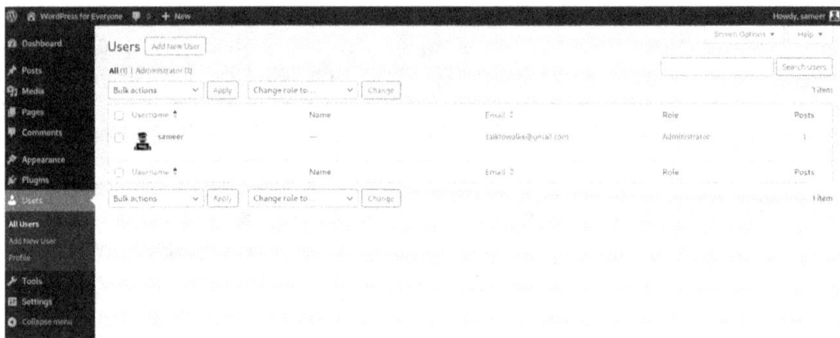

Fig. 4.11 Users

## Understanding User Roles

WordPress comes with several predefined user roles, each with different capabilities and access levels:

- **Administrator:** Has full access to all website features and settings.

- **Editor:** Can create, edit, publish, and manage all posts and pages, including those written by other users.

- **Author:** Can create, edit, and publish their own posts.

- **Contributor:** Can create and edit their own posts but cannot publish them.

- **Subscriber:** Can only read published content and manage their own profile.

Assigning appropriate roles to users ensures that individuals have the necessary access to perform their tasks while preventing unauthorized modifications to your website. For example, if you have guest bloggers contributing to your site, you can assign them the "Contributor" role, allowing them to write and edit posts but not publish them directly.

By effectively managing users and roles, you can maintain control over your website and ensure its smooth operation.

# 4.7 Settings and Configuration

The WordPress Settings section allows you to configure various aspects of your website, from basic information to advanced functionalities. Let's explore some of the key settings you can manage:

## General Settings

- **Site Title and Tagline:** Set your website's title and tagline, which are displayed in the browser tab and often in the website header.

- **WordPress Address (URL) and Site Address (URL):** These should typically be the same and reflect your website's domain name.

- **Email Address:** Set the website's primary email address for administrative purposes and notifications.

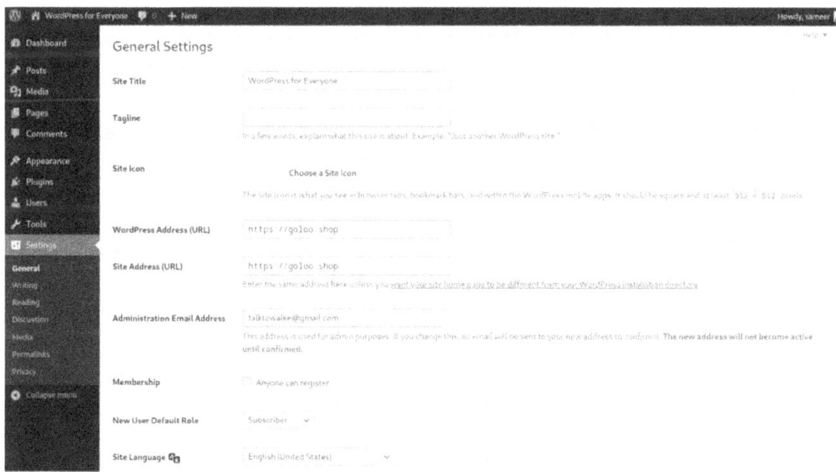

*Fig. 4.12 Settings*

- **Membership:** Enable or disable user registration on your website.

- **New User Default Role:** Choose the default user role assigned to new registered users.

- **Time Zone:** Set your website's time zone to ensure accurate time and date display.

- **Date Format and Time Format:** Choose your preferred date and time display formats.

- **Week Starts On:** Select the day that marks the beginning of the week on your website.

- **Permalink Structure:** Choose the structure of your website's URLs, which impacts SEO and user experience.

## Writing Settings

- **Default Post Category:** Select the default category assigned to new posts.

- **Default Post Format:** Choose the default format for new posts (e.g., standard, aside, gallery).

- **Post via email:** Configure settings for publishing posts via email.

- **Update Services:** Add URLs of services to be notified when you publish new content.

## Reading Settings

- **Your homepage displays:** Choose whether your homepage displays your latest posts or a static page.

- **Blog pages show at most:** Set the maximum number of posts displayed on your blog page.

- **Syndication feeds show the most recent:** Set the number of posts displayed in your RSS feed.

- **For each article in a feed, show:** Choose whether to display the full text or an excerpt in your RSS feed.

- **Search Engine Visibility:** Enable or disable search engine indexing of your website.

## Discussion Settings

- **Default comment settings:** Configure settings like comment moderation, nested comments, and comment author information requirements.

- **Other comment settings:** Manage settings related to comment blacklisting, avatars, and email notifications.

## Media Settings

- **Image sizes:** Set default image sizes for thumbnails, medium, and large images.

- **Uploading Files:** Configure settings related to file types allowed for upload and maximum upload file size.

## Permalinks Settings

- **Custom Structure:** Create a custom URL structure for your posts and pages.

- **Common Settings:** Most of Themes recommend "Post Name" as permalink structure to work properly.

**Remember:** Explore the various settings sections carefully and adjust them to match your website's specific needs and preferences.

## 4.8 Tools

The WordPress dashboard's Tools section acts as your website's utility belt, offering a variety of functionalities to manage and optimize your online presence. Let's delve into the common tools you might find:

- **Import:** This tool allows you to import posts, pages, comments, and even custom fields from various sources.

- **Export:** Need to create a backup of your website's content for safekeeping or migration purposes? The Export tool comes to the rescue. It lets you export your posts, pages, comments, custom fields, and even categories and tags in a downloadable format.

- **Privacy:** As data privacy regulations evolve, this tool empowers you to manage user privacy settings on your website. You can generate a file containing user information upon request and offer options for users to erase their data. In recent versions this option may have shifted to Settings>Privacy.

- **Available Tools:** This section might house a couple of hidden gems – scripts for specific tasks. These could include tools to convert categories to tags for improved organization or a "Press This" bookmarklet for effortless content creation from any webpage. (Availability depends on your theme and plugins)

**Note:** The specific tools available in your dashboard might vary depending on your WordPress theme and any installed plugins.

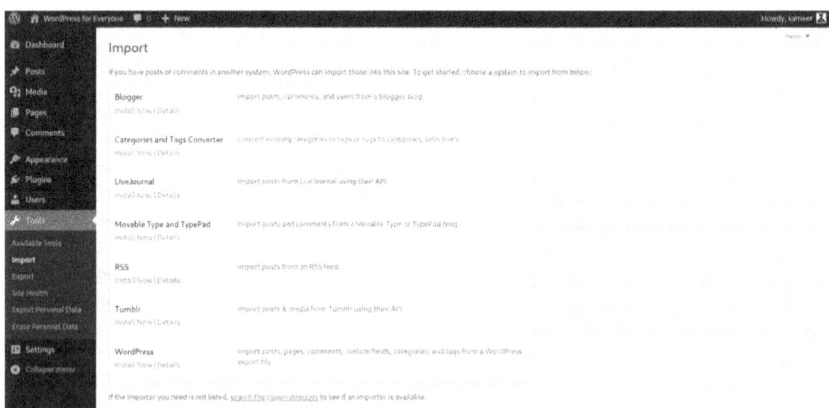

*Fig. 4.13 Tools Menu*

# 4.9 Conclusion

The WordPress Dashboard is your gateway to managing and customizing your website. By exploring its various sections and features, you gain the power to control your website's content, appearance, functionality, and security.

From creating and managing content to installing themes and plugins, the Dashboard provides a user-friendly interface for building and maintaining your website. Take some time to familiarize yourself with the different sections and experiment with the settings to tailor your website to your specific needs.

As you become more comfortable with the WordPress Dashboard, you'll unlock its full potential and gain the confidence to build and manage a website that truly reflects your vision.

***

# Chapter 5: Understanding WordPress Themes and Plugins

What will you learn:



## 5.1 Introduction

WordPress themes and plugins are the magic wands that allow you to transform your website from a basic template into a unique and functional online presence. They empower you to customize your website's appearance and add features without needing to touch a single line of code.

Think of **themes as the design architects** of your website. They control the overall look and feel, including the layout, colors, fonts, and overall aesthetic. With thousands of themes available, you can find one that perfectly matches your website's purpose and your personal style.

**Plugins**, on the other hand, are like **functional add-ons**. They extend your website's capabilities by adding specific features, such as contact forms, social media integration, SEO optimization, e-commerce functionality, and much more. There's a plugin for almost everything you can imagine, allowing you to build a website that perfectly meets your needs.

This chapter will guide you through the world of WordPress themes and plugins. We'll explore how to choose, install, and manage them effectively. You'll learn how to customize your website's appearance with themes and add powerful features with plugins. By the end of this chapter, you'll be equipped to unleash the full potential of WordPress and create a website that is truly your own.

# 5.2 WordPress Themes

WordPress themes are the foundation of your website's visual appearance. They control everything from the layout and colors to the fonts and overall aesthetic. Choosing the right theme is crucial for creating a website that is visually appealing, user-friendly, and reflects your brand or personal style.

## What are Themes?

Think of a theme as a pre-designed template for your website. It dictates the overall structure and visual elements, including:

- **Layout:** How your website content is arranged and displayed.

- **Colors and Fonts:** The color scheme and typography used throughout your website.

- **Header and Footer:** The design and content of your website's header and footer sections.

- **Images and Media:** How images and other media are displayed on your website.

- **Styling:** The overall visual style and aesthetic of your website.

## Choosing a Theme

With thousands of free and premium themes available, choosing the right one can feel overwhelming. Here are some key factors to consider:

- **Design:** Choose a theme with a design that aligns with your website's purpose and your brand identity.

- **Features:** Consider the features you need for your website and choose a theme that offers them or allows you to add them through plugins.

- **Responsiveness:** Ensure the theme is responsive, meaning it adapts and displays well on all devices, including desktops, tablets, and smartphones.

- **Compatibility:** Check if the theme is compatible with your current version of WordPress and any essential plugins you plan to use.

- **Reviews and Ratings:** Look at user reviews and ratings to gauge the theme's quality, support, and ease of use.

## Installing and Activating Themes

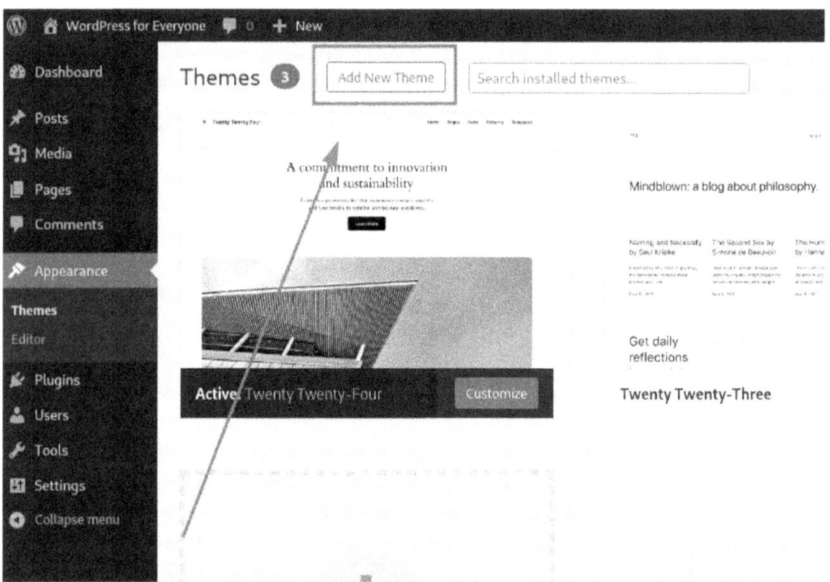


*Fig. 5.1: Click "Add New Theme" to search or upload a theme.*

You can install themes directly from the WordPress theme directory within your Dashboard. Simply navigate to Appearance > Themes (Fig. 5.1), browse the directory, and click "Install" on the theme you desire. Once installed, click "Activate" to make the theme live on your website.

## Customizing Themes

Most themes offer customization options through the WordPress Customizer. This user-friendly tool allows you to modify theme settings, colors, fonts, layouts, and other design elements in real-time, with a live preview of your changes.

The Appearance > Customize section lets you personalize your WordPress site's look and feel. Here are some key options:

- **Colors:** Change your site's primary and accent colors for a cohesive brand identity.

- **Background:** Set a background image, color, or pattern for a unique visual style.

- **Menus:** Create and manage navigation menus for easy website browsing.

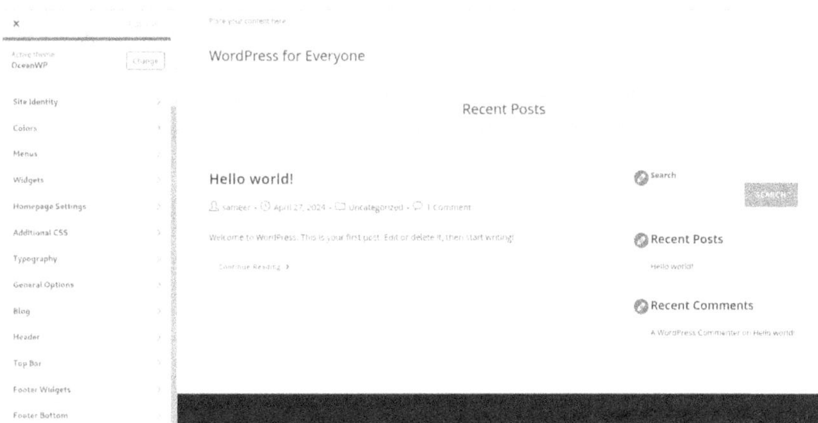

*Fig. 5.2 Customizer of OceanWP Theme*

- **Widgets:** Add interactive elements like calendars, search bars, and social media icons to sidebars or specific areas.

- **Header Image:** Set a custom image for your website's header for a more impactful introduction.

- **Site Identity:** Edit your site title, tagline, and logo – the basic building blocks of your brand.

These are just some of the most common options. Depending on your theme, you might find additional settings like font choices, layout controls, and even custom content sections.

## Child Themes

If you want to make significant customizations to a theme without affecting the original theme files, you can create a child theme. A child theme inherits the functionality and styling of the parent theme but allows you to make modifications without losing your changes when the parent theme is updated.

By carefully choosing and customizing a theme, you can create a website that is visually appealing, user-friendly, and reflects your unique brand or personality.

**Note:** Beginners can skip this for now! Child themes are an advanced way to customize your WordPress site. But if your theme offers them, here's the key: install the main theme first (it's the base). Then, install and activate the child theme.

# 5.3 WordPress Plugins

While themes control the visual appearance of your website, plugins are the workhorses that add functionality and features. They allow you to extend your website's capabilities without needing to code. Whether you want to add a contact form, optimize your website for SEO, or create an e-commerce store, there's a plugin for that!

## What are Plugins?

Plugins are essentially software extensions that integrate seamlessly with your WordPress website. They can add a wide range of features, including:

- **Contact forms:** Allow visitors to contact you directly through your website.

- **Social media integration:** Add social media buttons and feeds to your website.

- **SEO optimization:** Improve your website's search engine ranking.

- **E-commerce:** Create an online store and sell products or services.

- **Image galleries:** Showcase your images in beautiful galleries.

- **Security enhancements:** Protect your website from cyberattacks.

- **Performance optimization:** Make your website faster and more efficient.

## Finding and Choosing Plugins

The WordPress plugin directory offers a vast library of free plugins. You can also find premium plugins from third-party vendors. When choosing plugins, consider the following:

- **Functionality:** Does the plugin offer the features you need?

- **Compatibility:** Is the plugin compatible with your WordPress version and theme?

- **Reviews and Ratings:** Check user reviews and ratings to gauge the plugin's quality, support, and ease of use.

- **Developer Reputation:** Choose plugins from reputable developers with a track record of providing updates and support.

## Installing and Activating Plugins

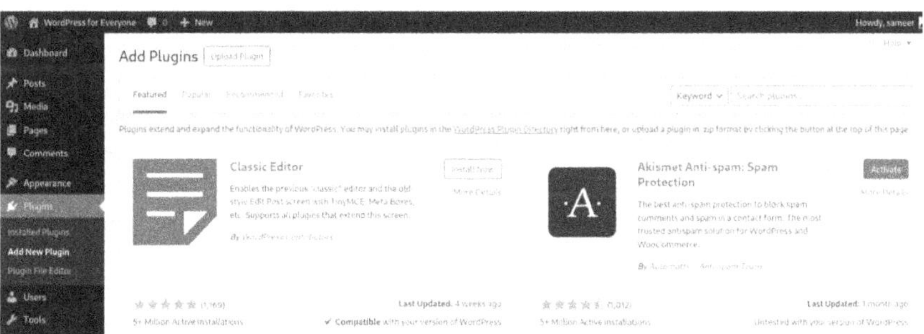

*Fig 5.3 Simply search or upload plugin to install and activate it.*

Similar to themes, you can install plugins directly from the WordPress plugin directory within your Dashboard. Navigate to Plugins > Add New, search for the desired plugin, and click "Install Now." Once installed, click "Activate" (Fig 5.3) to enable the plugin on your website.

## Managing Plugins

It's important to keep your plugins updated for security and compatibility. You can update plugins directly from the Dashboard. You can also deactivate or uninstall plugins that you no longer need or use.

## Popular Plugin Categories

Here are some popular plugin categories and their functionalities:

- **SEO:** Optimize your website for search engines to improve your ranking in search results.

- **Security:** Protect your website from cyberattacks and malware.

- **Performance:** Improve your website's loading speed and overall performance.

- **Social Media:** Integrate social media buttons, feeds, and sharing options on your website.

- **E-commerce:** Create an online store and sell products or services.

- **Contact Forms:** Allow visitors to contact you directly through your website.

By choosing and managing plugins effectively, you can add powerful features and functionalities to your WordPress website, making it more engaging and user-friendly.

# 5.4 Theme and Plugin Conflicts

While themes and plugins work together to enhance your website, conflicts can sometimes arise between them, leading to unexpected behavior or website errors. This section will help you identify and troubleshoot such conflicts.

## Identifying Conflicts

Common signs of theme and plugin conflicts include:

- **Website errors:** Error messages displayed on your website.

- **Broken layouts:** Elements of your website appearing distorted or misplaced.

- **Unexpected behavior:** Website features not working as expected.

- **Slow loading times:** Significant decrease in website performance.

## Troubleshooting Conflicts

Here are some steps you can take to troubleshoot theme and plugin conflicts:

1. **Deactivate all plugins:** This is the first step to isolate the issue. If the problem disappears after deactivating all plugins, then one of the plugins is likely causing the conflict.

2. **Reactivate plugins one by one:** Once you've deactivated all plugins, reactivate them one at a time, checking your website after each activation. This will help you identify the specific plugin causing the conflict.

3. **Switch to a default theme:** If deactivating plugins doesn't resolve the issue, try switching to a default WordPress theme like Twenty Twenty-Two. If the problem disappears, then your theme might be conflicting with a plugin or WordPress core.

4. **Update WordPress, themes, and plugins:** Ensure you're using the latest versions of WordPress, your theme, and all plugins. Updates often include bug fixes and compatibility improvements that can resolve conflicts.

5. **Check error logs:** If your website is experiencing errors, check your hosting provider's error logs for more specific information about the issue.

6. **Seek help:** If you're unable to resolve the conflict on your own,

consult the plugin or theme developer's support forums or seek help from the WordPress community.

**Remember:** It's important to keep your WordPress installation, themes, and plugins updated to minimize the risk of conflicts. Additionally, choosing well-coded and reputable themes and plugins from trusted sources can help prevent compatibility issues.

By following these troubleshooting steps, you can identify and resolve theme and plugin conflicts, ensuring a smooth and functional website experience for your visitors.

# 5.5 Best Practices for Using Themes and Plugins

While themes and plugins offer endless possibilities for customizing your WordPress website, it's important to use them strategically and responsibly. Here are some best practices to keep in mind:

## Choosing Quality Themes and Plugins

- **Prioritize well-coded and reputable themes and plugins:** Look for themes and plugins from trusted developers with a track record of providing updates and support. Check user reviews and ratings to gauge the quality and reliability of the theme or plugin.

- **Avoid themes and plugins from unreliable sources:** Downloading themes and plugins from untrusted sources can expose your website to security vulnerabilities and malware. Stick to the official WordPress theme and plugin directories or reputable third-party vendors.

## Keeping Themes and Plugins Updated

- **Update regularly:** WordPress, themes, and plugins receive regular updates that include security patches, bug fixes, and compatibility improvements. Keeping everything updated is crucial for maintaining a secure and functional website.

- **Enable automatic updates (Optional):** Consider enabling automatic updates for WordPress core and plugins to ensure you're always using the latest versions. However, it's recommended to manually update themes to avoid potential visual disruptions to your website.

## Managing Theme and Plugin Overload

- **Use only what you need:** While it's tempting to install numerous themes and plugins, using too many can negatively impact your website's performance and security. Only install and activate the themes and plugins that are essential for your website's functionality and design.

- **Deactivate and uninstall unused themes and plugins:** Regularly review your installed themes and plugins and deactivate or uninstall those you no longer use. This helps keep your website lean and efficient.

## Additional Tips

- **Test updates before applying them to your live website:** If you have a staging site or local development environment, test updates there before applying them to your live website. This helps ensure that updates don't cause any unexpected issues.

- **Take regular backups of your website:** Backups are essential for recovering your website in case of any unforeseen problems. Many hosting providers offer backup solutions, or you can use backup plugins.

By following these best practices, you can optimize your use of themes and plugins, ensuring a secure, high-performing, and well-maintained WordPress website.

# 5.6 Conclusion

WordPress themes and plugins are the dynamic duo that empowers you to create a website that is both visually stunning and highly functional. Themes shape the visual identity of your website, while plugins add features and extend its capabilities.

By understanding how to choose, install, and manage themes and plugins effectively, you unlock the full potential of WordPress. You can create a website that perfectly reflects your brand or personality and offers a seamless user experience.

Remember to prioritize quality, compatibility, and security when choosing themes and plugins. Keep everything updated, and avoid overloading your website with unnecessary additions. With careful planning and strategic use of themes and plugins, you can build a WordPress website that is truly exceptional.

This chapter concludes **Part 1: Getting Started With WordPress**. We've covered the essential steps to launch your WordPress journey, from choosing a hosting provider and domain name to installing WordPress and exploring the Dashboard. Now, equipped with the foundational knowledge and tools, you're ready to embark on the exciting process of building your website. In **Part 2,** we'll dive deeper into the **practical aspects of website creation**, guiding you through content creation, design customization, and adding powerful features to bring your website vision to life.

***

# Part 2

# Building Your Website

# Chapter 6: Creating and Editing Pages and Posts

What will you learn:



## 6.1 Understanding Pages and Posts

Before we dive into the creation process, let's clarify the difference between pages and posts:

- **Pages:** These are static content that remains relatively unchanged over time. Examples include your "About Us" page, "Contact" page, or product landing pages.

- **Posts:** These are dynamic content, typically displayed in reverse chronological order (newest first). Blog posts, news articles, and announcements are prime examples of posts.

Choosing the right format for your content is crucial. Here's a simple guideline:

### Use pages for

- Timeless information that rarely changes.

- Content that doesn't need to be categorized or tagged.

- Standalone content not part of a chronological series.

## Use posts for

- Timely and regularly updated content.

- Content you want to categorize or tag for easier navigation.

- Content that contributes to a chronological blog or news feed.

Understanding this distinction will help you organize your website effectively and ensure your content is presented in the most appropriate way.

# 6.2 Creating New Pages and Posts

Now that you understand the difference between pages and posts, let's create some content!

## Accessing the Editor

1. **For pages:** Hover over "Pages" in the left-hand menu and click "Add New."

2. **For posts:** Hover over "Posts" in the left-hand menu and click "Add New."

This will open the WordPress editor, where you'll craft your content.

## Using the Gutenberg Editor

WordPress utilizes the Gutenberg editor, a block-based system for creating content. Here's how to use it effectively:

1. **Blocks:**

   - Gutenberg offers various blocks for different content types, including text, images, videos, galleries, and more.

   - Click the "+" icon to add a new block and choose the

desired type.

- Each block has its own settings for customization. For example, you can adjust image size, alignment, and caption.

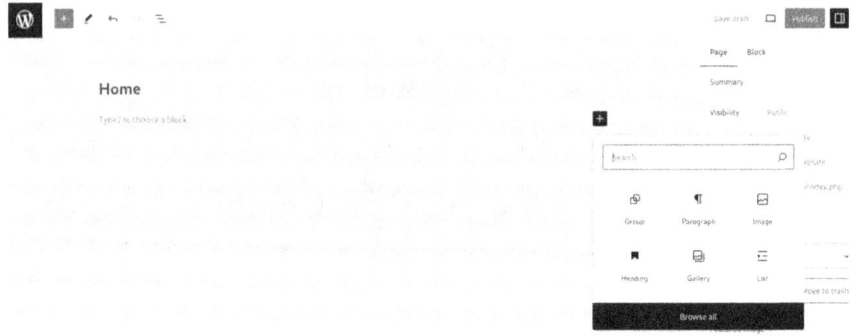

*Fig. 6.1 Exploring default page builder.*

## 2. Formatting Options:

- Use the toolbar above each block to format text, including bold, italics, headings, lists, and links.

- You can also access additional formatting options by clicking the three dots on the toolbar.

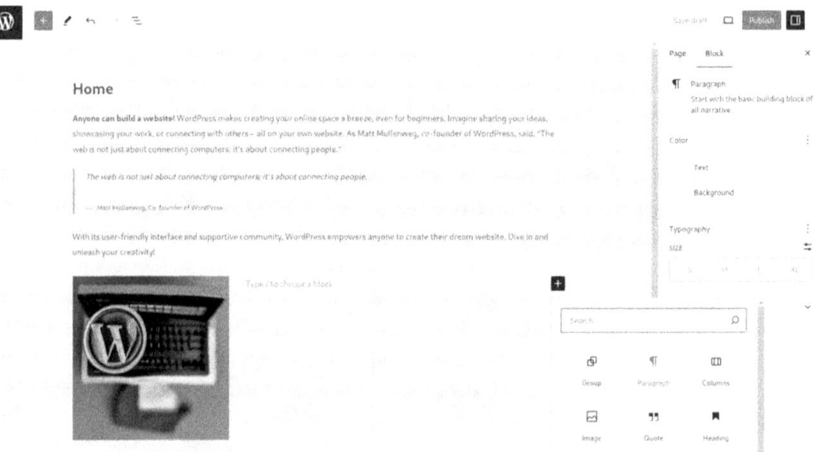

*Fig. 6.2 Designing the page with various block tools.*

### 3. Media Embeds:

- To embed images or other media, click the "+" icon and choose the appropriate block (e.g., "Image").

- You can upload files from your computer or select existing media from your media library.

## Publishing and Scheduling

- Once your content is ready, click the "Publish" button in the top right corner.

- You can also schedule your content for future publication by clicking the "Publish" dropdown and selecting "Schedule."

**Remember:** You can preview your page or post before publishing by clicking the "**Preview**" button.

After publishing a page, you might notice that widgets occupy an additional third of the page (Fig. 6.5). These widgets are typically displayed in sidebars, which can appear on every page by default depending on your theme settings. While sidebars are useful for adding information to blog posts, they're generally not used for static pages. To remove the sidebar from your page, navigate to **Appearance > Customize** in your WordPress dashboard and look for the appropriate settings.

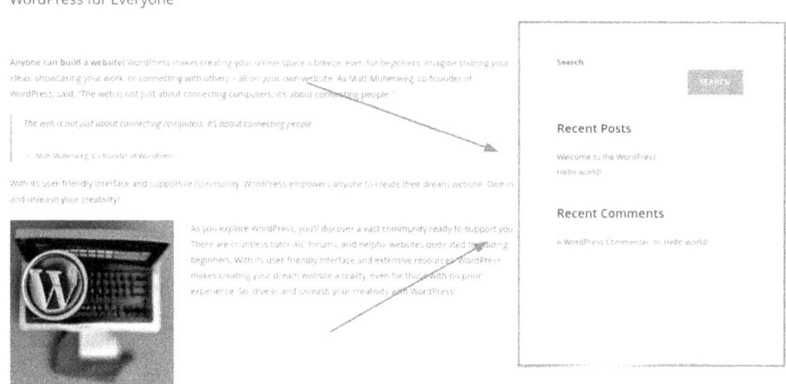

*Fig. 6.3 Static page with default sidebar.*

# 6.3 Editing Existing Pages and Posts

*Fig. 6.4 Editing a page.*

Even the best content sometimes needs a little tweaking. Here's how to edit existing pages and posts:

## Accessing the Editor for Existing Content

1. For pages: Go to "Pages" > "All Pages."

2. For posts: Go to "Posts" > "All Posts."

3. Find the page or post you want to edit and click its title or the "Edit" link below it (Fig. 6.6).

This will open the Gutenberg editor with your existing content.

## Editing Text and Media

- You can edit existing text directly within the relevant blocks.

- To edit media, click on the media element and use the settings panel to make changes. You can also replace the media with a different file.

## Revision History and Revisions

- WordPress automatically saves revisions of your content as you work.

- Click the "Revisions" button in the top right corner to see the revision history.

- You can compare revisions and restore to a previous version if needed.

**Remember:** Always save your changes by clicking the "Update" button after editing.

By utilizing these features, you can easily keep your website content up-to-date and error-free.

# 6.4 Page and Post Settings

Beyond the content itself, several settings can enhance your pages and posts:

## Titles and Permalinks

- **Title:** This is the main heading of your page or post and is crucial for SEO and user experience. Choose a clear and concise title that accurately reflects your content.

- **Permalink:** This is the unique URL of your page or post. WordPress automatically generates a permalink based on your title, but you can edit it for better readability and SEO.

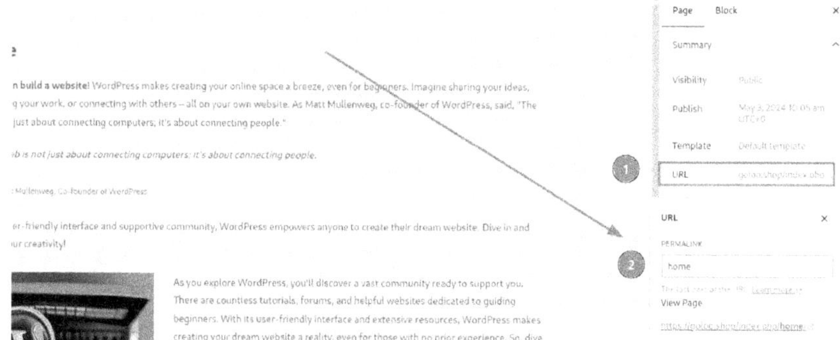

*Fig. 6.5 Editing page URL or Permalink.*

## Featured Images

Featured images act as tiny previews for your content, appearing on your homepage, blog feed, and even search results. Choose one that visually represents your post, grabbing attention and giving visitors a hint of what to expect.

## Categories and Tags

- **Categories:** These help organize your content into broad topics. For example, a blog might have categories like "News," "Reviews," and "Tutorials."

- **Tags:** These are more specific keywords that describe your content. For example, a blog post about a new phone might be tagged with "technology," "smartphone," and "review."

## Additional Settings

- **Author Attribution:** You can choose to display or hide the author of the page or post.

- **Comments:** You can enable or disable comments for individual pages and posts.

- **Page/Post Visibility:** You can control who can see your content by setting it to "Public," "Private," or "Password Protected."

**Remember:** Optimizing these settings will improve your website's organization, navigation, and SEO.

# 6.5 Setting a homepage

By default, WordPress is a dynamic platform, but you can achieve a static feel for specific pages. For that you need to set a homepage. There are two main ways to set a homepage:

1. **Using Settings:** Navigate to Settings > Reading. Under "Your homepage displays," choose "A static page" from the dropdown menu. Select the page you want as your homepage and, optionally, choose another for your blog posts (if applicable).

2. **Using Customize:** Head to Appearance > Customize. Many themes offer options to hide unnecessary elements on specific pages. Explore these settings to refine the static website look for your chosen pages.

Remember, this approach creates a static feel for specific pages, but doesn't convert your entire WordPress site to pure static HTML.

# 6.6 Tips and Best Practices

Here are some tips and best practices to keep in mind when creating and editing pages and posts:

## Writing Effective Content

- **Know your audience:** Write content that is relevant and engaging for your target audience.

- **Focus on clarity and conciseness:** Use clear language and avoid jargon. Get to the point quickly and avoid unnecessary fluff.

- **Structure your content:** Use headings, subheadings, and paragraphs to break up your text and improve readability.

- **Incorporate keywords:** Use relevant keywords throughout your content to improve search engine optimization (SEO). However, avoid keyword stuffing, which can harm readability and SEO.

## Optimizing for Readability

- **Use short sentences and paragraphs:** This makes your content easier to read and digest.

- **Utilize bullet points and numbered lists:** This helps break up text and highlight key points.

- **Choose readable fonts and font sizes:** Ensure your text is easy to read on all devices.

- **Use white space effectively:** Don't overcrowd your content with text and images.

## Using Visuals Effectively

- **Choose high-quality images and media:** This will enhance the visual appeal of your content.

- **Optimize image sizes:** Large images can slow down your

website. Use image editing tools to optimize image sizes before uploading them.

- **Use captions and alt text:** This provides context for your images and improves accessibility for visually impaired users.

- **Place images strategically:** Images should complement your content and not distract from it.

By following these tips, you can create content that is not only informative but also engaging and visually appealing.

## 6.7 Conclusion

Congratulations! You've mastered the art of creating and editing pages and posts in WordPress.

You can now confidently build your website's content, whether it's informative pages, engaging blog posts, or anything in between. Remember to utilize the Gutenberg editor's features effectively, optimize your content for readability and SEO, and keep your website fresh with regular updates.

As you continue your WordPress journey, explore different content formats, experiment with various blocks and media embeds, and refine your writing skills. With practice and creativity, you'll craft a website that not only informs but also captivates your audience.

Now, let's move on to the next chapter and explore the exciting world of working with images and media in WordPress!

***

# Chapter 7: Working with Images and Media

What will you learn:



## 7.1 Introduction

Images and media are essential elements of any website, bringing your content to life and enhancing the user experience. In this chapter, we'll explore everything you need to know about working with images and media in WordPress.

We'll cover uploading files to your Media Library, optimizing images for performance, inserting media into your content, and managing your media files effectively. By the end of this chapter, you'll be equipped to create a visually appealing and engaging website with optimized media performance.

## 7.2 Uploading Images and Media

The Media Library is your central hub for managing all your website's images, videos, and other media files. Let's explore how to upload files to your Media Library:

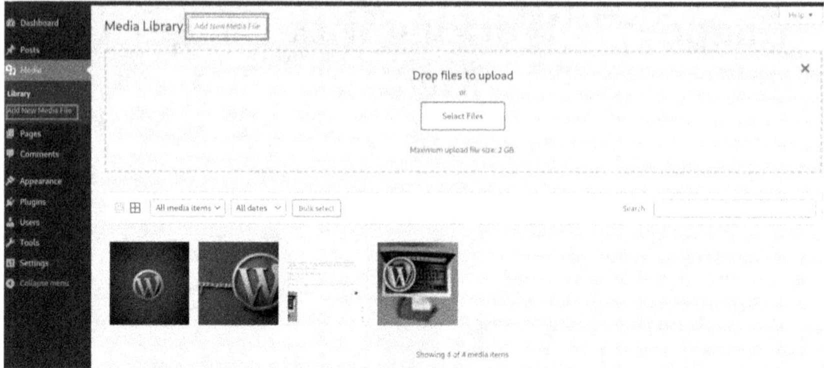


*ig. 7.1 Directly uploading files to media library*

## Accessing the Media Library

1. Log in to your WordPress dashboard.

2. Click on "Media" in the left-hand menu. This will open the Media Library.

## Uploading Files

1. Click the "Add New" button at the top of the Media Library.

2. You can either drag and drop files directly into the upload area or click the "Select Files" button to browse your computer.

3. Once you've selected your files, click the "Open" button to upload them.

## Understanding File Types and Formats

WordPress supports a wide range of file types, including images (JPEG, PNG, GIF), videos (MP4, MOV), audio (MP3, WAV), and documents (PDF, DOCX). Ensure your files are in a compatible format before uploading.

## Adding Metadata

Once you've uploaded your files, take a moment to add some metadata to them. This information acts like a digital label, enriching your media and making it more discoverable. Here's a breakdown of the key metadata fields:

- **Title:** Give your file a clear and descriptive title that accurately reflects its content. This helps you easily identify it later and improves searchability within your media library.

- **Caption:** Craft a short sentence or two that provides additional context for the image. This caption can appear below the image on your website, offering viewers a deeper understanding of its content.

- **Alt Text:** This hidden gem plays a crucial role in accessibility and SEO. Write a concise description of the image's content, as this text is displayed for visually impaired users and gets picked up by search engines.

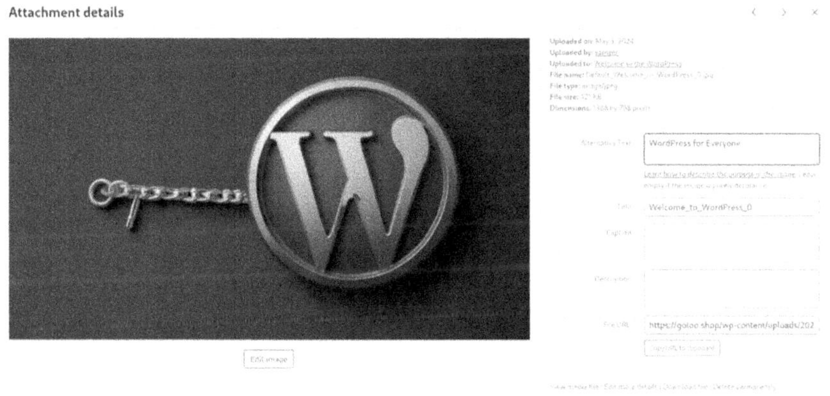

*7.2 Adding metadata details to an image file.*

By investing a few minutes in adding metadata, you'll be organizing your media library for efficient future use, enhancing accessibility for all visitors, and potentially boosting your website's search engine ranking.

## 7.3 Inserting Images and Media into Content

Now that you have your images and media uploaded to the Media Library, let's explore how to insert them into your content:

*Fig. 7.3 Adding a media file into a post.*

## Inserting Images and Media

1. Open the page or post where you want to insert the media.

2. Click the "+" icon to add a new block.

3. Choose the appropriate block for your media type (e.g., "Image" for images, "Video" for videos).

4. You can either upload a new file from your computer or select an existing file from your Media Library.

## Alternative Method

You can also insert media using the "Add Media" button above the editor toolbar. This allows you to insert media into existing blocks or create new blocks with the selected media.

## Aligning and Positioning Images

Most image blocks offer alignment options (e.g., left, center, right) and allow you to adjust the image size. Experiment with these settings to achieve the desired layout for your content.

## Adding Captions and Alt Text

- **Captions:** These appear below the image and provide additional context.

- **Alt Text:** This describes the image for visually impaired users and search engines. It's important to add descriptive alt text to all your images for accessibility and SEO.

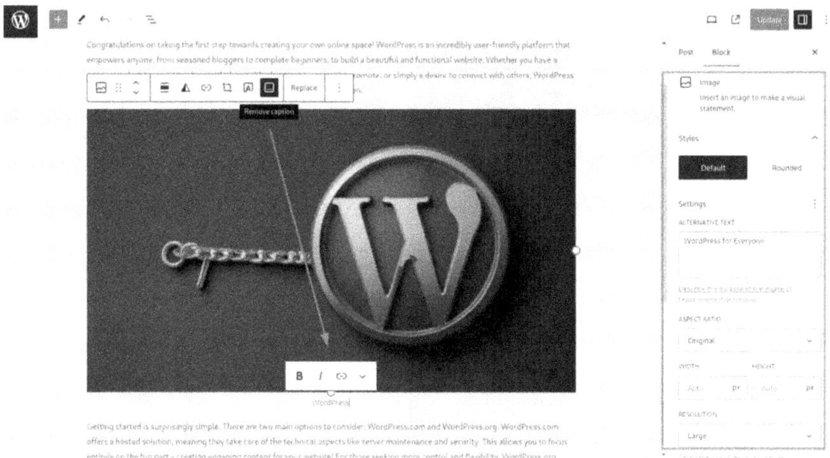

*Fig. 7.4 Additional options for an image.*

**Remember:** You can edit the settings of your inserted media by clicking on the media element and using the settings panel that appears.

By following these steps, you can seamlessly integrate images and media into your content, enhancing its visual appeal and engagement.

# 7.4 Media Library Management

As your website grows, your Media Library can become quite extensive. Here are some tips for managing your media files effectively:

## Organizing and Categorizing

- **Create folders:** You can create folders within the Media Library to organize your files by topic, date, or any other system that works for you.

- **Use categories:** WordPress allows you to assign categories to your media files, making it easier to find specific types of media.

## Searching and Filtering

- Use the search bar in the Media Library to find specific files by name or keyword.

- You can also filter your media files by type, date, or category.

## Deleting and Restoring Media Files

- To delete a media file, hover over it and click the "Delete Permanently" link.

- If you accidentally delete a file, you can restore it from the "Trash" folder within the Media Library.

### Additional Tips

- **Use descriptive filenames:** This will help you easily identify your files in the Media Library.

- **Delete unused media files:** Regularly clean up your Media Library by deleting files you no longer use. This will help improve website performance.

By following these tips, you can keep your Media Library organized and efficient, making it easy to find and manage your media files.

# 7.5 Tips and Best Practices

Here are some essential tips and best practices to keep in mind when working with images and media on your WordPress website:

## Choosing High-Quality Images and Media

- **Use high-resolution images:** This ensures your images look sharp and clear, especially on high-resolution screens.

- **Select relevant and engaging media:** Choose images and videos that complement your content and enhance the user experience.

- **Consider image composition and aesthetics:** Pay attention to the visual elements of your images, such as lighting, color, and framing.

## Optimizing Image Sizes

- **Resize images before uploading:** Large images can slow down your website. Use image editing tools to resize images to the appropriate dimensions before uploading them to WordPress.

- **Compress images:** Image compression reduces file size without significantly impacting image quality. Use online tools or plugins to compress your images before or after uploading.

## Using Captions and Alt Text Effectively

- **Write descriptive captions:** Captions provide context for your images and can enhance understanding for your readers.

- **Always add alt text:** Alt text describes the image for visually impaired users and search engines. Use clear and concise language to describe the image content and its purpose.

## Avoiding Copyright Infringement

- **Use royalty-free images or purchase licenses:** Ensure you have the right to use the images and media you include on your website.

- **Give proper attribution:** If required, credit the source of the image or media file.

By following these tips, you can ensure your website uses high-quality, optimized images and media that enhance your content and provide a positive user experience.

# 7.6 Conclusion

Remember to choose high-quality images, optimize them for performance, and use captions and alt text effectively. By following these best practices, you'll ensure your website provides a positive user experience and ranks well in search engine results.

***

# Chapter 8: Adding Navigation and Menus

What will you learn:



## 8.1 Understanding WordPress Menus

Navigation menus are essential for guiding visitors through your website and helping them find the information they need. In WordPress, menus provide a structured way to organize and display links to your pages, posts, categories, and even external websites.

### Types of Menus

WordPress allows you to create multiple menus for different purposes, such as:

- **Primary Menu:** This is the main navigation menu, typically displayed at the top of your website.

- **Footer Menu:** This menu is often located in the footer of your website and may include links to less prominent pages, such as your privacy policy or terms of service.

- **Social Media Menu:** This menu contains links to your social media profiles.

### Importance of Clear Navigation

Clear and intuitive navigation is crucial for a positive user experience. Visitors should be able to easily find the information they're looking for without feeling lost or frustrated. Well-designed menus help achieve this by:

- **Providing a logical structure:** Menus should be organized in a way that makes sense to users, with related pages grouped together.

- **Using clear and descriptive labels:** Menu labels should be concise and accurately reflect the content of the linked page.

- **Prioritizing important pages:** The most important pages on your website should be prominently featured in your menus.

By understanding the role and importance of menus, you can create a navigation system that enhances the usability and effectiveness of your website.

## 8.2 Creating and Managing Menus

Now that you understand the importance of menus, let's dive into creating and managing them in WordPress:

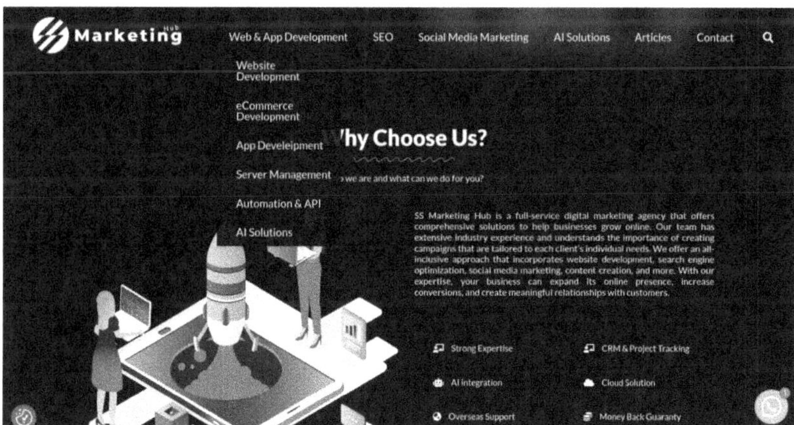



*Fig. 8.1 Primary/main menu of our marketing agency*

### Creating a New Menu

1. Log in to your WordPress dashboard.

2. Go to "Appearance" > "Menus".

3. Click on the "create a new menu" link.

4. Give your menu a name (e.g., "Main Menu") and click the "Create Menu" button.

## Adding Menu Items

1. On the left-hand side, you'll see panels for different types of content you can add to your menu, such as Pages, Posts, Custom Links, and Categories.

2. Select the desired content type and check the boxes next to the items you want to add.

3. Click the "Add to Menu" button.

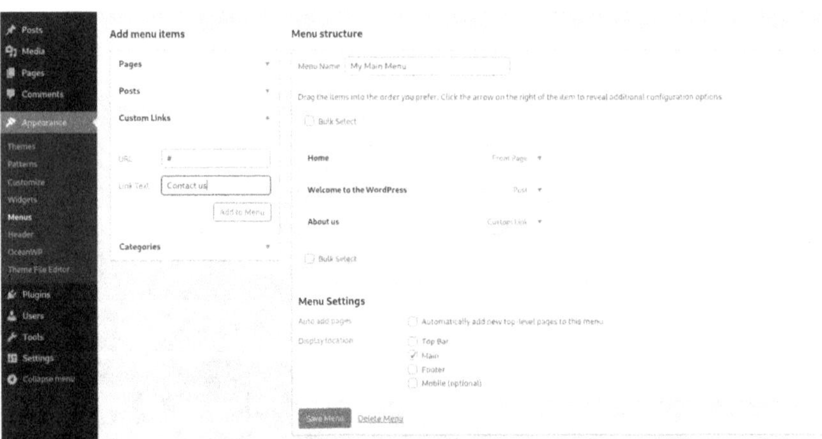

*Fig. 8.2 Adding items and links to the main menu.*

## Arranging Menu Items

● You can easily rearrange menu items using drag-and-drop functionality. Simply click and hold on a menu item and drag it to the desired position.

● To create sub-menus, drag a menu item slightly to the right, under another menu item. This will create a nested structure.

## Additional Options

- You can edit the navigation label for each menu item.

- You can also add custom CSS classes to menu items for further styling.

## Saving Your Menu

- Once you're satisfied with your menu, click the "Save Menu" button.

**Remember:** You can create multiple menus for different purposes and assign them to different menu locations in your theme.

By following these steps, you can create and manage menus that provide a clear and intuitive navigation experience for your website visitors.

# 8.3 Menu Locations and Display

WordPress themes typically define specific areas where menus can be displayed. These areas are called "menu locations."

## Understanding Menu Locations

- Different themes offer different menu locations. Common locations include the header, footer, sidebar, and below the header.

- The available menu locations for your theme can be found in the "Manage Locations" tab on the Menus page.

## Assigning Menus to Locations

1. Go to "Appearance" > "Menus".

2. Click on the "Manage Locations" tab.

3. For each menu location, select the desired menu from the dropdown list.

4. Click the "Save Changes" button.

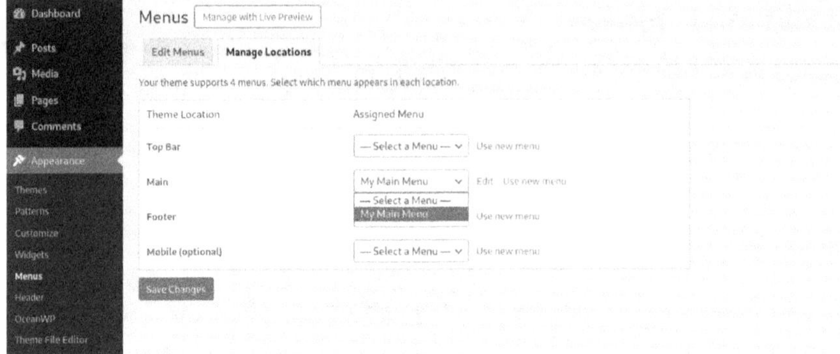

*Fig. 8.3 Managing the menu locations.*

## Controlling Menu Display

- Some themes offer options to control the display of menus on different devices (e.g., desktop, mobile).

- You may be able to choose different menus for different devices or adjust the menu styles for optimal viewing on smaller screens.

- These options can usually be found in the theme customizer or theme settings.

## Additional Considerations

- **Menu Depth:** Consider the depth of your menus, especially on mobile devices. Too many levels of sub-menus can be difficult to navigate.

- **Menu Styles:** The appearance of your menus will depend on your theme's styles. You may be able to customize menu colors, fonts, and spacing using the theme customizer or custom CSS.

By understanding menu locations and display options, you can ensure your menus are displayed effectively and contribute to a positive user experience on all devices.

# 8.4 Adding Custom Links and Categories to Menus

In addition to pages and posts, you can also add custom links and categories to your menus (Fig. 8.3) for enhanced navigation:

## Adding Custom Links

1.  Go to "Appearance" > "Menus".

2.  Click on the "Custom Links" panel on the left-hand side.

3.  In the "URL" field, enter the full URL of the website or page you want to link to.

4.  In the "Link Text" field, enter the text that will be displayed in the menu.

5.  Click the "Add to Menu" button.

## Adding Categories

1.  Go to "Appearance" > "Menus".

2.  Click on the "Categories" panel on the left-hand side.

3.  Check the boxes next to the categories you want to add to the menu.

4.  Click the "Add to Menu" button.

## Uses for Custom Links and Categories

- **Linking to external websites:** You can add links to social media profiles, partner websites, or other relevant resources.

- **Linking to specific sections within your website:** You can create custom links to anchor points on a page or to specific sections of your website that don't have their own page.

- **Providing easy access to content categories:** Adding categories to your menu allows users to easily browse content within specific topics.

**Remember:** You can arrange custom links and categories within your menu just like any other menu item using drag-and-drop functionality.

By incorporating custom links and categories, you can create more comprehensive and user-friendly navigation menus for your website.

## 8.5 Tips and Best Practices

Creating effective navigation menus requires careful planning and consideration. Here are some tips and best practices to keep in mind:

### Menu Structure and Organization

- **Keep menus concise:** Avoid overwhelming users with too many menu items. Focus on the most important pages and categories.

- **Use clear and descriptive labels:** Menu labels should be easy to understand and accurately reflect the content of the linked page.

- **Organize menus logically:** Group related pages together and use sub-menus to create a hierarchical structure.

- **Prioritize important pages:** Place the most important pages at the beginning or end of your menu, as these are the areas users tend to focus on.

### Menu Design and Usability

- **Ensure mobile responsiveness:** Test your menus on different devices to ensure they are easy to navigate on smaller screens.

- **Use clear visual hierarchy:** Use font sizes, colors, and spacing to create a visual hierarchy that guides users through the menu.

- **Consider accessibility:** Ensure your menus are accessible to users with disabilities by using appropriate color contrast and providing alternative navigation methods.

### Additional Tips

- **Use drop-down menus sparingly:** Too many levels of sub-menus can be confusing and difficult to navigate.

- **Test your menus regularly:** As your website evolves, make sure your menus remain relevant and easy to use.

- **Get feedback from users:** Ask friends, family, or colleagues to test your website's navigation and provide feedback.

By following these tips and best practices, you can create navigation menus that are both user-friendly and effective in guiding visitors through your website.

## 8.6 Conclusion

Navigation menus play a crucial role in guiding visitors through your website and ensuring they can easily find the information they need. By understanding the different types of menus, creating and managing them effectively, and following best practices for menu design and usability, you can create a navigation system that enhances the user experience and contributes to the success of your website.

Remember, clear and intuitive navigation is essential for keeping visitors engaged and encouraging them to explore your content. As you continue to develop your website, regularly review and refine your menus to ensure they remain effective and meet the needs of your audience.

***

# Chapter 9: Customizing Your Website with Widgets

What will you learn:



## 9.1 What are Widgets?

Widgets are like building blocks for your website, allowing you to add content and functionality to different areas without needing to code. They offer a simple and flexible way to customize your website's layout and enhance the user experience.

Imagine widgets as small modules that you can drag and drop into designated areas of your website, such as sidebars, footers, or even within your content. These modules can display various types of content, including:

- **Text:** Add custom text, such as a welcome message, contact information, or a call to action.

- **Images:** Showcase images or create image galleries.

- **Videos:** Embed videos from YouTube, Vimeo, or other platforms.

- **Social Media Feeds:** Display your latest social media posts.

- **Calendars:** Show upcoming events or appointments.

- **Search Bars:** Make it easy for visitors to find content on your website.

- **And much more!**

*Fig. 9.1 Search (1), Recent Posts (2), Recent Comments (3) and Calendar (4) widgets are used in this sidebar.*

WordPress comes with a variety of built-in widgets, and many **themes and plugins offer additional widgets** with even more functionality. By using widgets strategically, you can create a website that is both informative and engaging for your visitors.

## 9.2 Available Widgets in WordPress

WordPress comes with a variety of built-in widgets that you can use to add content and functionality to your website. Here are some of the most common widgets:

- **Archives:** Displays a monthly archive of your posts.

- **Calendar:** Shows a calendar of your posts.

- **Categories:** Lists your post categories.

- **Custom HTML:** Allows you to add custom HTML code to your widget area.

- **Gallery:** Displays an image gallery.

- **Meta:** Provides links to login, RSS feeds, and WordPress.org.

- **Navigation Menu:** Displays a navigation menu.

- **Recent Comments:** Shows a list of recent comments.

- **Recent Posts:** Displays a list of your most recent posts.

- **Search:** Adds a search bar to your widget area.

- **Tag Cloud:** Displays a cloud of your most used tags.

- **Text:** Allows you to add text or HTML content.

## Additional Widgets from Themes and Plugins

Many themes and plugins offer additional widgets with even more functionality. For example, you might find widgets for:

- **Social media feeds:** Display your latest posts from Facebook, Twitter, Instagram, etc.

- **Email opt-in forms:** Collect email addresses from your visitors.

- **Testimonials:** Showcase positive feedback from your customers.

- **E-commerce products:** Display featured products or product categories.

The available widgets will vary depending on your theme and the plugins you have installed.

# 9.3 Adding and Managing Widgets

Adding and managing widgets in WordPress is a simple drag-and-drop process:

## Accessing the Widgets Page

Go to "Appearance" > "Widgets" (Fig. 9.2).

# Adding Widgets

1. On the Widgets page, you'll see a list of available widgets on the left-hand side and your widget areas on the right-hand side.

2. To add a widget, simply drag it from the left-hand side and drop it into the desired widget area.

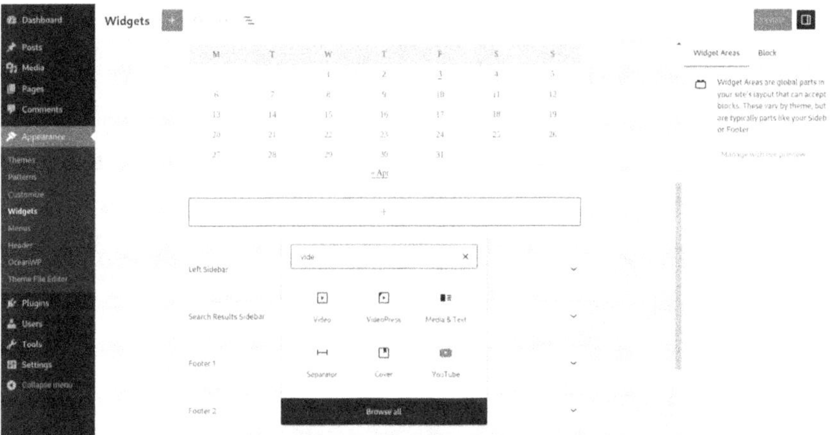

*Fig, 9.2 Adding a widget into the default sidebar.*

3. Once you've added a widget, you can configure its settings by clicking on the down arrow in the top right corner of the widget.

## Managing Widgets

- **Reorder widgets:** You can rearrange widgets within a widget area by dragging and dropping them.

- **Remove widgets:** To remove a widget, click on the down arrow in the top right corner and select "Remove".

- **Customize widget settings:** Each widget has its own settings that you can customize. For example, you can change the title of the widget, the number of items to display, or the appearance of the widget.

## Saving Changes

- Once you've made changes to your widgets, click the "Save" button at the bottom of the widget area.

**Remember:** The available widget areas and their locations will vary depending on your theme.

By using widgets effectively, you can add valuable content and functionality to your website without needing to code.

## 9.4 Widget Areas and Customization

Widget areas are designated sections within your WordPress theme where you can place widgets. The number and location of widget areas vary depending on the theme you are using.

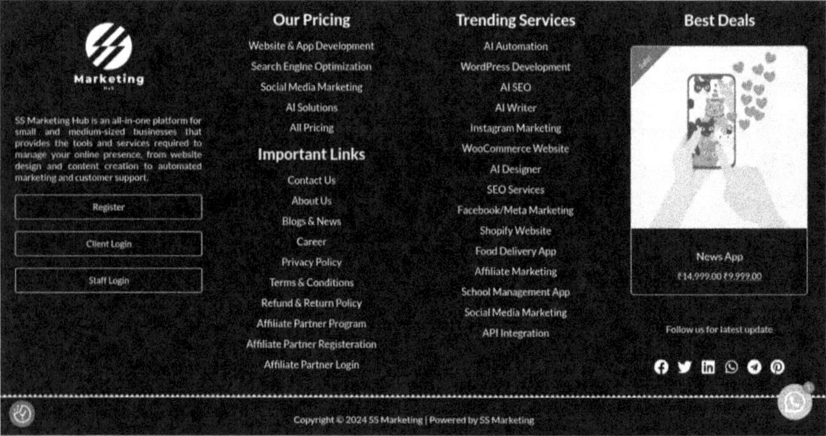

*Fig. 9.3 Footer Widgets Areas of our marketing agency website.*

## Common Widget Areas

- **Sidebar:** This is the most common widget area, typically located on the left or right side of your content.

- **Footer:** Many themes have multiple widget areas in the footer, allowing you to add content such as contact information, social media links, or a copyright notice.

- **Header:** Some themes have widget areas in the header, which can be used for navigation menus, search bars, or social media icons.

- **Content Area:** Some themes allow you to add widgets within your content area, such as between blog posts or inside bars within individual pages.

## Customizing Widget Areas

- **Theme Options:** Some themes offer options to customize the layout and appearance of widget areas (Fig. 9.4). You may be able to change the number of columns, the width of the widget area, or the background color.

*Fig. 9.4 Using Customizer to manage widgets with live preview.*

- **Plugins:** There are plugins available that allow you to create custom widget areas or modify existing ones.

- **Custom Code:** If you are comfortable with coding, you can use CSS to customize the appearance of your widget areas.

**Remember:** When customizing widget areas, it's important to consider the overall design and usability of your website. Avoid overcrowding widget areas with too many widgets, and ensure that the widgets you use are relevant to your content and audience.

By understanding widget areas and customization options, you can create a website layout that is both visually appealing and functional.

# 9.5 Tips and Best Practices

Here are some tips and best practices for using widgets effectively on your WordPress website:

## Choosing the Right Widgets

- **Relevance:** Select widgets that are relevant to your content and audience. Don't just add widgets for the sake of filling space.

- **Functionality:** Choose widgets that provide valuable functionality to your website, such as search bars, social media feeds, or email opt-in forms.

- **Visual Appeal:** Consider the visual design of your widgets and ensure they complement the overall look and feel of your website.

## Widget Placement and Layout

- **Prioritize important widgets:** Place the most important widgets in prominent locations, such as the top of your sidebar or footer.

- **Balance content and whitespace:** Avoid cluttering widget areas with too many widgets. Leave some whitespace to improve readability and visual appeal.

- **Consider mobile responsiveness:** Ensure your widgets look good and function properly on all devices, including smartphones and tablets.

## Additional Tips

- **Use widget titles effectively:** Widget titles should be clear and descriptive, helping users understand the purpose of the widget.

- **Customize widget settings:** Take advantage of the customization options available for each widget to tailor its appearance and functionality to your needs.

- **Test and iterate:** Experiment with different widget combinations and layouts to find what works best for your website.

By following these tips and best practices, you can use widgets to enhance your website's functionality, improve user experience, and achieve your website goals.

## 9.6 Conclusion

Widgets offer a powerful and flexible way to customize your WordPress website and enhance its functionality. By understanding what widgets are, exploring the available options, and following best practices for their use, you can create a website that is both informative and engaging for your visitors.

Remember to choose widgets that are relevant to your content and audience, prioritize their placement for maximum impact, and customize their settings to achieve your desired look and feel. With a little experimentation and creativity, you can use widgets to transform your website into a dynamic and user-friendly platform that effectively serves your online goals.

***

# Chapter 10: Advance Techniques and Methods

What will you learn:



## 10.1 Introduction

Welcome to the exciting world of advanced WordPress techniques! In this chapter, we'll venture beyond the basic setup and explore powerful tools and methods to take your website to the next level.

Here's what you can expect to learn:

- **Unlocking New Possibilities:** We'll start by discussing what "advanced techniques" mean in the context of WordPress. You'll understand how these tools allow you to personalize your website and make it truly your own.

- **Building a Strong Foundation:** Before diving into fancy customizations, we'll revisit the fundamental concept of website structure. We'll explore how pages, posts, categories, and tags work together to create a well-organized and user-friendly website.

- **A Gradual Approach:** Remember, going "advanced" doesn't mean becoming overwhelmed! We'll introduce advanced techniques gradually, ensuring you feel confident and in control throughout the process.

By the end of this chapter, you'll be equipped with the knowledge and resources to explore the advanced features of WordPress and unleash the full potential of your website. So, buckle up and get ready to take your website design skills to the next level!

## 10.2 Page Layouts

Each individual page within your website also has its own structure, which refers to the layout of its content. Imagine a well-designed room with designated areas for furniture. There are several common page layout styles:

1. **Left-Sidebar:** This classic layout features the main content area on the right with a sidebar on the left (Fig. 10.1), often used for menus, widgets, or additional information.

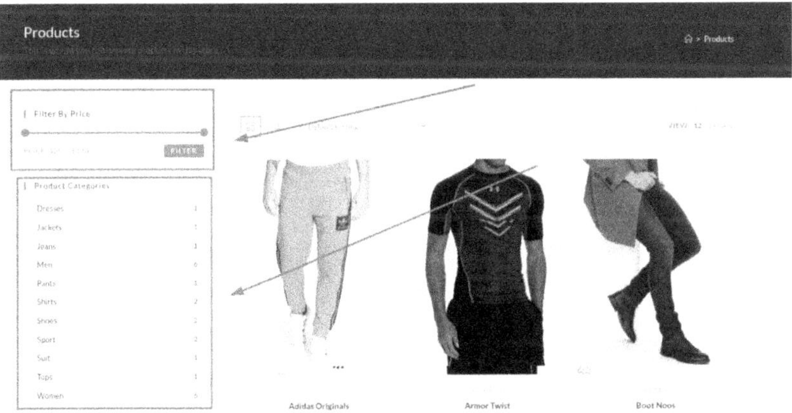


*Fig. 10.1 Most of ecommerce website use left sidebar*

2. **Right-Sidebar:** Similar to the left-sidebar layout, but with the sidebar positioned on the right (Fig. 9.1).

3. **Full-Width:** This layout maximizes the content area, often used

for landing pages (Fig 6.5 and 8.1) or portfolios.

4.  **Split-Screen:** This layout divides the page into two distinct sections, useful for showcasing contrasting content or products.

**Optimizing Your Structure**

By understanding both website and page structure, you can create a user-friendly and visually appealing website. This chapter will delve deeper into:

- **Choosing the right website structure:** We'll explore structures for blogs, portfolios, and e-commerce sites.

- **Optimizing your navigation:** Learn how to create menus that reflect your website structure.

- **Crafting compelling page layouts:** Explore different layout styles and choose the one that best suits your content.

By mastering page structure, you'll create a solid foundation for a website that delights both visitors and search engines.

# 10.3 Extending WordPress Limits

WordPress sets some default limits on the size of files you can upload. This might not be an issue for smaller websites, but if you want to showcase high-resolution images, infographics, or lengthy videos, you'll need to explore ways to increase these limits. Here's how to break free and upload larger files with confidence:

First, let's get familiar with the restrictions. By default, WordPress often limits uploads to around 2MB. This can be too small for high-quality media.

1.  **Access your website's root directory:** Use an FTP client or your web hosting provider's file manager to access the directory where your WordPress files are stored (usually named `public_html` or similar)(Fig, 3.5).

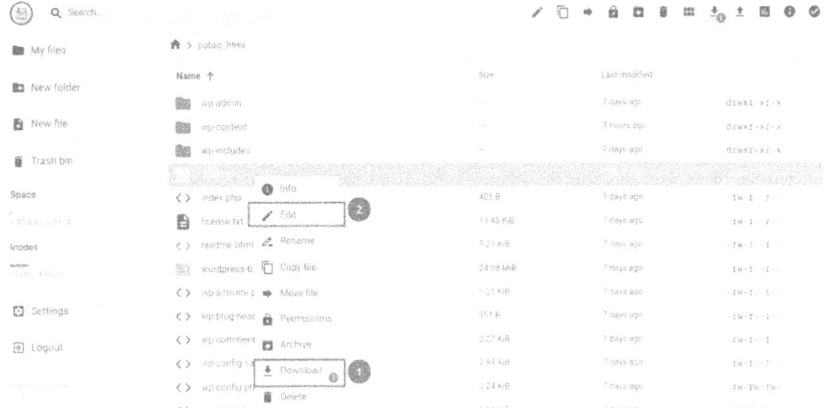

*Fig. 10.2 Download the .htaccess file for backup and click on edit.*

2. **Locate the ".htaccess" file:** This file might be hidden by default. Goto settings, find something related to 'hide' or 'hidden' and uncheck it.

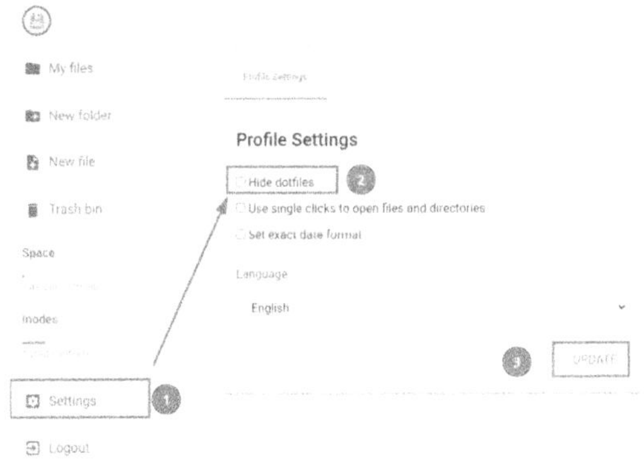

*Fig. 10.3 Uncheck 'hide dotfiles' and update the settings.*

3. **Edit the ".htaccess" file: Important:** Always create a backup (Fig 10.2) of the .htaccess file before making any changes.

Use a text editor to add the following code snippet **at the end** of the file (mostly after '# END WordPress'):

```
php_value upload_max_filesize 128M

php_value post_max_size 128M

php_value max_execution_time 300

php_value max_input_time 300
```

**Note:** In above code, 'M' stands for MB and time is mentioned in seconds. You can adjust the above numbers as per your requirement.

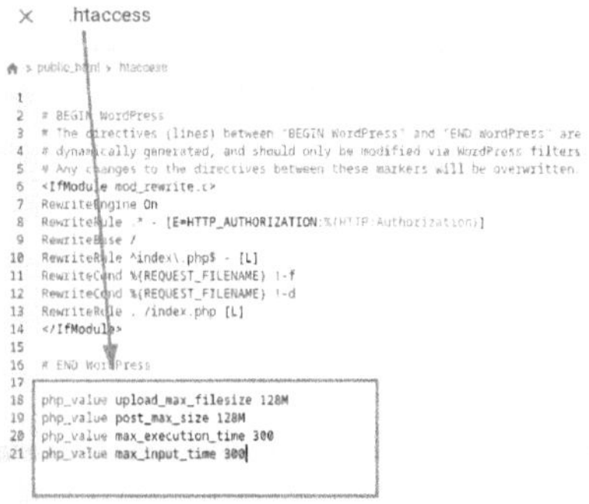

*Fig. 10.4 Editing .htaccess file to increase limits.*

4.  **Save the changes:** Make sure to save the modified `.htaccess` file back to your website's root directory.

**Note:** While modifying `.htaccess` can work, it's not the best choice for most users. Using plugins or contacting your hosting provider are generally safer and more beginner-friendly alternatives.

# 10.4 Advance Page Builders

While the Gutenberg editor offers a good foundation, there are several user-friendly alternatives available that may suit your preferences. Mastering Gutenberg will give you a solid understanding of most page builders due to their shared core functionalities.

Here are some popular options to consider:

- **Elementor:** This widely used plugin provides live editing and intuitive drag-and-drop tools (Fig. 10.5) for easy layout creation.

- **WPBakery Page Builder:** This premium plugin is often bundled with themes and offers both live and backend editing options.

- **SeedProd:** This versatile page builder allows you to create landing pages, coming soon pages, and more.

- **Beaver Builder:** Known for its speed and performance, Beaver Builder is a popular choice for those comfortable with some code.

- **Divi:** This feature-rich builder offers a visually oriented approach to design with a focus on beautiful premade layouts.

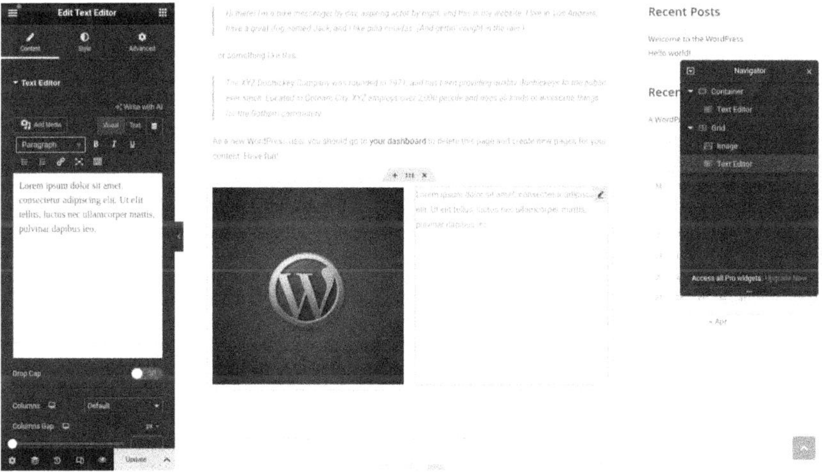

*Fig. 10.5 Using Elementor Page builder.*

This list is not exhaustive, and many other page builders exist. Exploring different options will help you find the one that best suits your comfort level and design needs.

## 10.5 Premade Demo Content

If you want to replicate the look and feel of your theme's preview quickly, demo content offers a shortcut. Many themes provide you with demo content to save time while creating an entire website from scratch. Think of it as a template, 'Demo content' offers beautiful, pre-built layouts often populated with sample content. Importing it saves you the effort of crafting layouts from scratch.

## Benefits

- **Faster Design:** Get a head start with a strong visual foundation.

- **Inspiration Spark:** Demos can ignite your creative juices for further customization.

- **Learning Tool:** See best practices for layout, content organization, and structure.

**Note:** Demos are starting points. You'll need to replace sample content with your own.

## Importing Demos

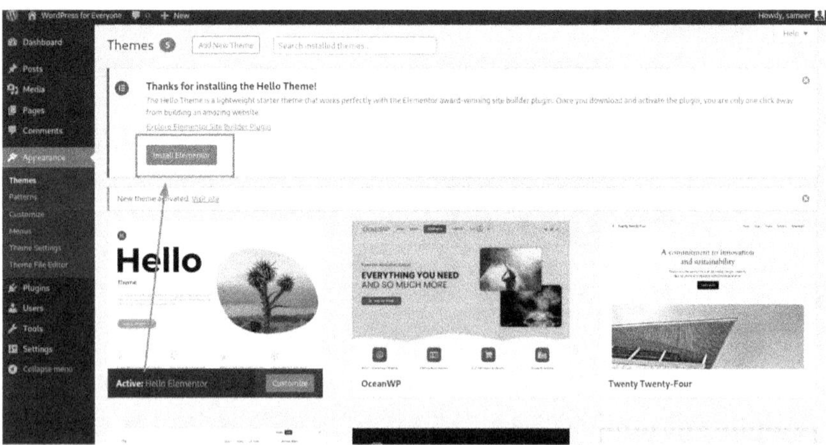

*Fig. 10.6 Message to 'Install Elementor' comes after activating 'Hello Elementor' Theme.*

Importing a demo is mostly common for every theme, but still if you find documentation related to your theme, you must verify if there is any variation of method. There are basically two main methods to import demo:

## 1. Theme Default

If your theme provides demos, then there must be a default method to import them. You should follow this method to get the best results:

a. **Install and Activate Required Plugins:** Check for the message (Fig. 10.6) that comes after activating your theme. It will ask you to install some recommended plugins. Click on that link and start installing those plugins. This is the most important step before you start importing any demo.

b. **Find a Demo Importer:** Sometimes themes provide their own demo importer, and sometimes they use external plugins. So, depending on that, the location of the demo importer varies. It's mostly visible in "Theme Settings > Import Demos" or "Appearance > Demo Import." If you're unable to find it, you must check your theme documentation. After opening the demo import, it may show multiple demo options. You can also check previews before installing them.

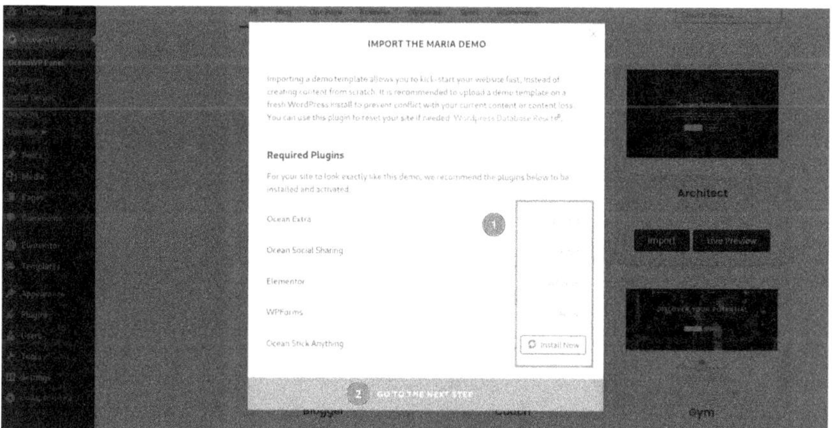

*Fig. 10.7 Installing and activating directly through demo import of OceanWP Theme*

c. **Check Compatibility:** The demo importer may check if you have installed the recommended plugins and for compatibility

(Fig. 10.7) with your WordPress version. You must have all required plugins installed to run the import smoothly.

d. **Import the Demo:** After checking compatibility, run the demo import (Fig. 10.8). It will take some time to import, so be patient while it completes. After a successful import, a message will appear prompting you to check your site.

**Note:** Some themes may provide external links or additional pages in their demo. Please edit all content.

By using demo content strategically, you can significantly reduce design time and get a stunning website up and running quickly. It's a launchpad, not the finish line! Use it as inspiration to build a website that reflects your unique brand.

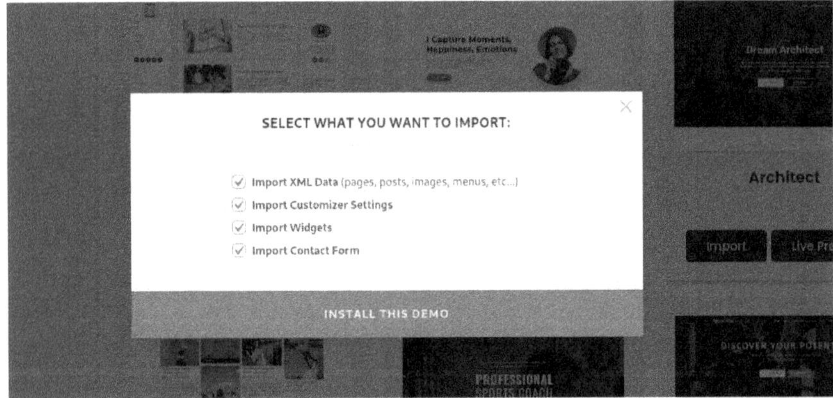


*Fig. 10.8 Final screen before demo import starts.*

## 10.6 Website Migration

Understanding website migration is crucial. It's the process of transferring your website's files and database from one location to another. This might be necessary in several situations:

- **From Local Server to Live Hosting:** Developed your website locally and want it live on the internet? Migration gets your website onto a live hosting server.

- **Changing Hosting Providers:** Unhappy with your current hosting provider? Website migration ensures a smooth transition to a new one.

- **Changing Domain:** Decided on a new domain name or subdomain? Migration moves your website to the new address while preserving content and functionality.

While the specific methods might differ slightly, the overall approach for migrating a WordPress website in these scenarios remains largely similar. Here, we'll explore two main methods for website migration:

# 1. Migration Plugins

Migration plugins offer the easiest way to move your website. While free versions of these plugins might have limitations, they simplify the process significantly. Let's explore some popular options and their free version limitations, followed by a step-by-step walkthrough using one of them.

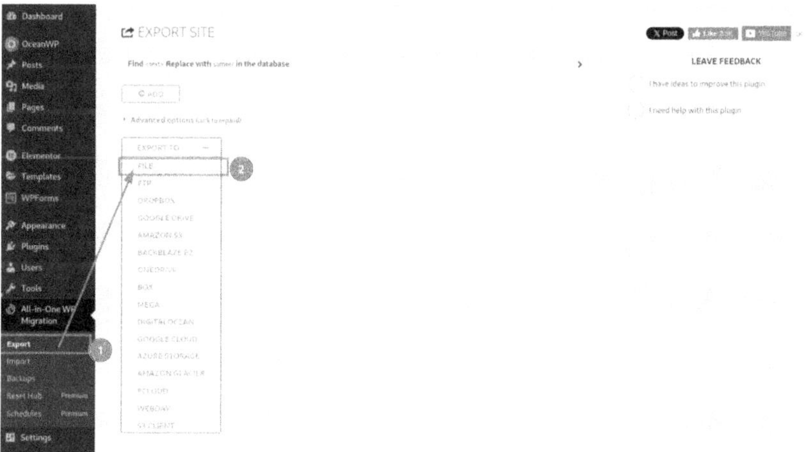


*Fig. 10.9 Exporting website using 'All-in-One WP Migration' plugin.*

**Popular Migration Plugins :**

- **All-in-One WP Migration and Backup**

- **UpdraftPlus**

- **Duplicator**

These plugins typically follow a similar process:

## a) Exporting Your Website:

1.  Install and activate the migration plugin on your existing website.

2.  Locate the export option within the plugin settings (Fig. 10.9). Some plugins might offer different export methods, but as a beginner, we recommend exporting as a "File."

3.  Initiate the export process. Be patient, as the export time depends on your website size. A single file will be generated upon completion. Download this file.

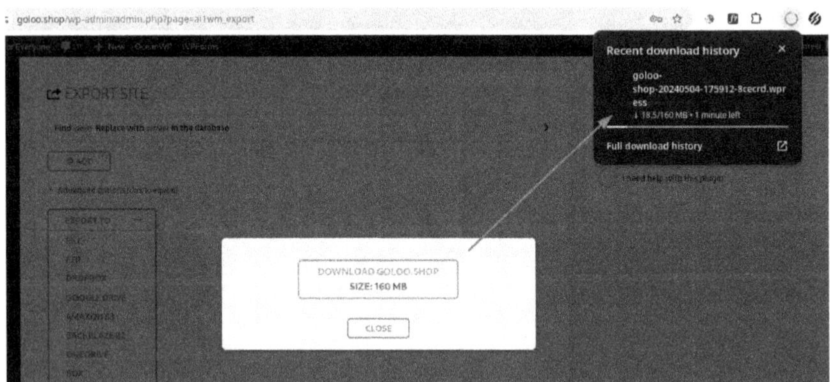

*Fig. 10.10 Download the exported file.*

## b) Importing Your Website:

1.  Log in to your new hosting location.

2.  Install and activate the same migration plugin you used in step a).

3.  Navigate to the plugin's import settings and upload the

downloaded export file.

4.  The import process will start automatically. Wait until it's
    complete..

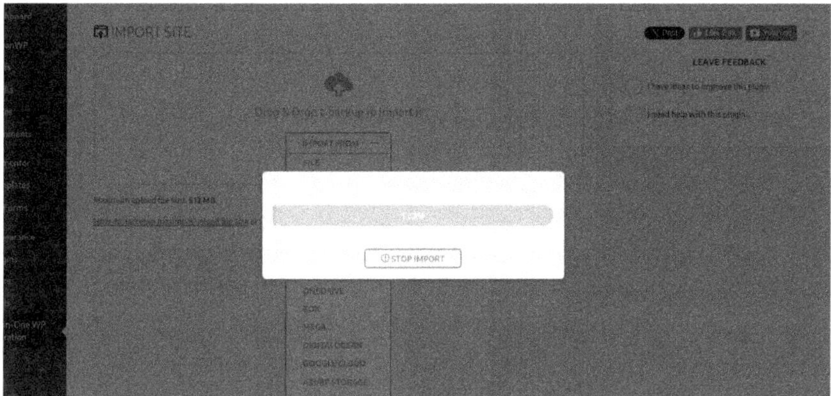

*Fig. 10.11 Importing a website into a new location*

**Note:** After the import, carefully review your website to ensure everything functions properly. Minor customization might be needed in some cases.

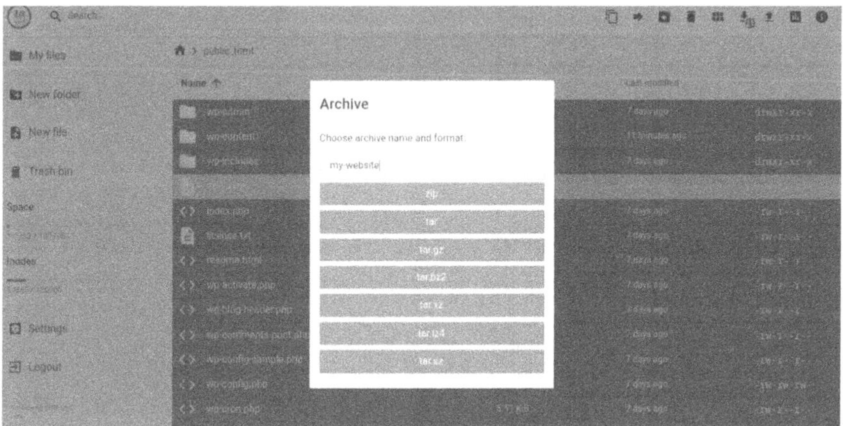

*Fig. 10.12 Creating a zip file to upload it in a new location.*

# 2. Manual Migration

While migration plugins offer a user-friendly approach, manual migration provides more control and flexibility. However, it requires more technical knowledge and is recommended for advanced users only. Here's a step-by-step guide:

## 1. Exporting Website Files:

- Access the file manager of your website you want to migrate.

- Select all files within the WordPress installation directory (typically named "public_html" or "www").

- Compress the selected files into a ZIP archive (Fig. 10.12). Download this ZIP file to your computer.

*Fig. 10.13 Entering phpMyAdmin, a software to manage databases.*

## 2. Exporting the Database:

- Access phpMyAdmin (Fig. 10.13), a tool for managing your website's database.

- Select the database associated with your WordPress website.

- Locate the export tab and keep the default settings. Initiate the export process. This will create a database file that will automatically download to your computer.

## 3. Importing on the New Location:

- Access the new hosting server and create a new database, user, and password. Note this information for later use.

*Fig. 10.14 Exporting a database from the phpMyAdmin*

- Open phpMyAdmin on the new server and select your newly created database.

- Click on the "Import" tab and upload the database file you downloaded earlier. This will import all your website's database content.

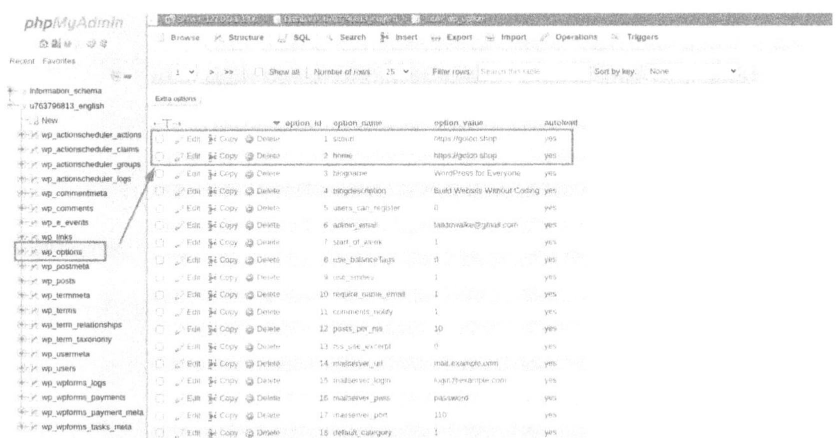

*Fig. 10.15 Modifying database tables for the new domain.*

## 4. Updating Database Configuration:

- If you're changing your domain name, you'll need to modify some database settings (Fig. 10.15).

- Locate the table named "wp_options" within your database list.

- Edit the "siteurl" and "home" entries within this table to reflect your new domain name.

**5. Uploading and Configuring Website Files:**

- Access the file manager on the new server. Upload the ZIP file containing your website files and extract it.

- Locate the "wp-config.php" file within the extracted files.

- Edit this file to update the database connection information. Replace the existing details with the database name, user, and password (Fig. 10.16) you created in step 3. This ensures your WordPress installation connects to the new database.

**Remember:** Website migration is an advanced task that you might encounter rarely. However, understanding both plugin-based and manual methods equips you with valuable knowledge. You can also use the FTP client to manage the WordPress files.

*Fig. 10.16 Editing 'wp-config.php' file to connect to the new database.*

# 10.7 Conclusion

This chapter ventured beyond WordPress basics, empowering you to customize and control your website's design. We explored website structure, different layouts, and optional features like demo content, larger file uploads, and website migration.

Here we conclude Part 2 of this book. You've been equipped with a solid foundation in WordPress and explored techniques for taking your website to the next level. In the next part, we'll delve into creating specific types of websites, guiding you through the process of building websites tailored for different purposes.

***

# Part 3
# Creating Different Types of Websites

# Chapter 11: Building a Blog or News Website

What will you learn:



## 11.1 Introduction

Blogs and news websites are powerful platforms for sharing your thoughts, ideas, and information with the world. Whether you're a passionate individual, a small business, or a large organization, WordPress provides the tools and flexibility to create a compelling and engaging online presence.

In this chapter, you'll explore the key steps involved in building a successful blog or news website using WordPress. We'll begin by discussing the importance of choosing the right theme and essential plugins that enhance functionality. Then, we'll delve into creating and managing blog posts, cffcctivcly catcgorizing and tagging your contcnt, and engaging your audience with interactive features.

*Fig. 11.1 Demo Homepage of a technology news site by OceanWP*

You'll also explore strategies for promoting your blog or news website and attracting a wider readership. Finally, we'll share valuable tips and best practices to help you create a thriving online platform that informs, inspires, and connects with your audience.

Get ready to embark on your blogging or news publishing journey and share your voice with the world!

## 11.2 Choosing the Right Theme

The theme you choose for your blog or news website plays a crucial role in its overall appearance and functionality. Here are some key factors to consider when selecting a theme:

- **Design and Layout:** Look for a theme with a clean and modern design that aligns with your brand and content. Consider the layout options, such as the number of columns, sidebar placement, and header styles.

- **Responsiveness:** Ensure the theme is responsive and adapts seamlessly to different screen sizes, providing a consistent user experience across desktops, tablets, and mobile devices.

- **Features and Functionality:** Choose a theme that offers features specifically designed for blogs or news websites, such as post formats, featured images, author bios, and social media integration.

- **Customization Options:** Look for a theme that allows you to customize colors, fonts, layouts, and other design elements to match your brand identity.

- **Performance and Speed:** Choose a theme that is well-coded and optimized for performance to ensure fast loading times and a smooth user experience.

## Popular Theme Options

*Fig. 11.2 Demo Homepage of a personal blogging site by OceanWP*

- **Free Themes:** WordPress offers a wide selection of free themes in the official theme directory. These themes are a great starting point, especially for beginners.

- **Premium Themes:** Premium themes offer more advanced features, customization options, and support. Popular theme marketplaces include ThemeForest, Elegant Themes, and StudioPress.

**Remember:** The right theme can enhance the visual appeal, functionality, and user experience of your blog or news website. Take your time to explore different options and choose a theme that aligns with your goals and vision.

# 11.3 Essential Plugins for Blogs and News Websites

Plugins are like apps for your WordPress website, adding extra features and functionality. Here are some essential plugins to consider for your blog or news website:

## SEO Optimization

- **Yoast SEO:** This popular plugin helps you optimize your content for search engines, improving your website's visibility in search results.

- **Rank Math SEO:** Another comprehensive SEO plugin with features for keyword optimization, schema markup, and more.

**Note:** Use any one SEO plugin, if you activate multiple plugins, they may create conflict with each other.

## Content Enhancement

- **WPForms:** Create contact forms, surveys, and other types of forms to engage with your audience.

- **MonsterInsights:** Connect your website to Google Analytics and gain insights into your website traffic and user behavior.

- **Akismet Anti-Spam:** Protect your website from spam comments.

## Social Media Integration

- **Social Sharing Plugin – Social Warfare:** Add social sharing buttons to your content, making it easy for readers to share your posts on social media platforms.

- **Smash Balloon Social Photo Feed:** Display your Instagram feed on your website.

## Performance Optimization

- **WP Super Cache:** Improve website speed and performance by caching your pages and posts.

- **Smush:** Optimize images to reduce file size and improve loading times.

## Additional Plugins

- **Editorial Calendar:** Plan and schedule your blog posts with a visual calendar.

- **Related Posts:** Display related posts at the end of each article to keep readers engaged.

- **Mailchimp for WordPress:** Integrate your website with Mailchimp to build an email list and send newsletters.

**Remember:** Choose plugins that address your specific needs and avoid overloading your website with too many plugins, which can impact performance.

# 11.4 Creating and Managing Blog Posts.

Creating engaging and informative blog posts is essential for attracting and retaining readers. Here's a guide to creating and managing your blog content:

## Creating Good Blog Posts

- **Craft your content:** Use your favorite page editor to add text, images, videos, and other elements to your post.

- **Optimize for readability:** Use headings, subheadings, bullet points, and short paragraphs to make your content easy to read.

- **Incorporate visuals:** Include images, infographics, or videos to enhance your content and engage readers.

- **Optimize for SEO:** Use relevant keywords throughout your post and optimize your title and meta description.

*Fig. 11.3 Demo of a blog post design with featured image and sidebar*

## Managing Blog Posts

- **Categories and Tags:** Organize your posts using categories and tags for easy navigation and searchability.

- **Featured Images:** Set a featured image for each post to create a visually appealing thumbnail in your blog feed.

- **Excerpts:** Write a brief excerpt for each post to summarize its content and entice readers to click through.

- **Revisions:** Utilize the revision history feature to track changes and revert to previous versions if needed.

- **Scheduling:** Schedule posts to be published at specific times or dates.

## Post Formats

WordPress offers various post formats, such as **standard, aside, gallery, and quote**. Choose the format that best suits your content.

## Additional Tips

- **Write consistently:** Publish new content regularly to keep your audience engaged.

- **Promote your posts:** Share your posts on social media and other platforms to reach a wider audience.

- **Engage with your readers:** Respond to comments and encourage discussion.

By following these guidelines, you can create and manage high-quality blog posts that attract readers and establish your website as a valuable source of information.

# 11.5 Categorizing and Tagging Your Content

Organizing your blog posts with categories and tags is crucial for improving navigation and searchability, making it easier for readers to find the content they're interested in.

*Fig 11.4 Demo categories of a Travel Blogging website.*

## Categories

- Categories are like broad topics that group your posts into main themes. For example, a food blog might have categories like "Recipes," "Restaurant Reviews," and "Cooking Tips."

- Use categories to create a high-level structure for your content.

- Keep the number of categories manageable to avoid

overwhelming readers.

## Tags

- Tags are more specific keywords that describe the content of individual posts. For example, a recipe post might be tagged with "pasta," "vegetarian," and "Italian."

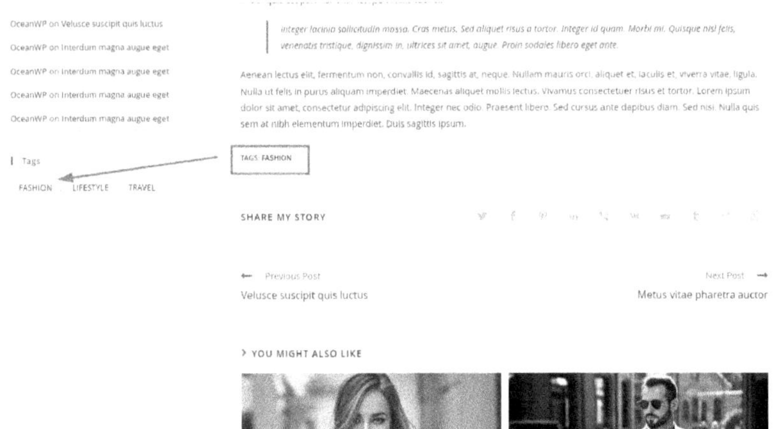

Fig. 11.5 Tags used at the bottom of th e page.

- Use tags to provide additional context and detail about your posts.

- You can use multiple tags for each post.

## Best Practices for Categorizing and Tagging

- **Be consistent:** Use a consistent set of categories and tags across your blog posts.

- **Choose relevant terms:** Select categories and tags that accurately reflect the content of your posts.

- **Avoid redundancy:** Don't create categories and tags that are too similar.

- **Use a hierarchical structure:** Consider creating subcategories within main categories for further organization.

## Benefits of Effective Categorization and Tagging

- **Improved navigation:** Readers can easily browse content within specific categories or topics.

- **Enhanced searchability:** Search engines can better understand the content of your website and improve your search rankings.

- **Increased engagement:** Readers can discover related content through categories and tags, keeping them engaged with your website.

By effectively categorizing and tagging your content, you create a well-organized and user-friendly blog or news website that caters to the interests of your audience.

# 11.6 Engaging Your Audience

Building a loyal and engaged audience is crucial for the success of your blog or news website. Here are some strategies to foster reader engagement:

## Encourage Comments and Discussion

- **Enable comments:** Allow readers to leave comments on your posts and respond to their feedback.

- **Ask questions:** Encourage discussion by asking questions at the end of your posts.

- **Moderate comments:** Monitor comments for spam and inappropriate content.

## Social Media Interaction

- **Share your posts on social media:** Promote your content on platforms like Facebook, Twitter, and Instagram.

- **Engage with your followers:** Respond to comments and messages, and participate in relevant conversations.

- **Run social media contests or giveaways:** Encourage interaction and attract new followers.

## Email Marketing

- **Build an email list:** Offer an email newsletter to keep readers updated on your latest content.

- **Send regular newsletters:** Share your latest blog posts, news, and exclusive content with your subscribers.

- **Personalize your emails:** Segment your audience and send targeted emails based on their interests.

## Interactive Content

- **Create polls and surveys:** Gather feedback from your audience and encourage participation.

- **Host webinars or live Q&A sessions:** Connect with your readers in real-time and answer their questions.

- **Embed quizzes or interactive infographics:** Make your content more engaging and fun.

## Community Building

- **Create a forum or online community:** Provide a space for readers to connect and discuss topics related to your website.

- **Host events or meetups:** Bring your audience together in person to build relationships and foster a sense of community.

**Remember:** Building an engaged audience takes time and effort. Be consistent, provide valuable content, and interact with your readers to foster a loyal following.

# 11.7 Promoting Your Blog or News Website

Creating great content is only half the battle. To attract readers and grow your audience, you need to actively promote your blog or news website. Here are some effective promotion strategies:

## Search Engine Optimization (SEO)

- **Optimize your content for relevant keywords:** Use keyword research tools to identify keywords that your target audience is searching for.

- **Optimize your website structure and meta tags:** Ensure your website is easy for search engines to crawl and index.

- **Build backlinks:** Get other websites to link to your content, which can improve your search engine rankings.

## Social Media Marketing (SMM)

- **Share your content on social media platforms:** Promote your blog posts and news articles on Facebook, Twitter, LinkedIn, and other relevant platforms.

- **Engage with your followers:** Respond to comments, answer questions, and participate in conversations.

- **Run social media ads:** Target your ideal audience with paid advertising campaigns.

## Content Collaboration

- **Guest blogging:** Write guest posts for other blogs in your niche to reach a new audience.

- **Collaborate with other bloggers or influencers:** Partner with others to create joint content or cross-promote each other's work.

## Other Promotion Strategies

- **Submit your website to directories:** List your website in relevant online directories.

- **Participate in online communities:** Engage in forums and online groups related to your niche.

- **Attend industry events:** Network with other professionals and potential readers.

**Remember:** Promoting your blog or news website is an ongoing process. Experiment with different strategies and track your results to see what works best for your audience.

## 11.8 Tips and Best Practices

Here are some additional tips and best practices to help you build a successful blog or news website:

### Content Quality

- **Focus on providing value:** Create content that is informative, engaging, and relevant to your audience.

- **Maintain high editorial standards:** Ensure your content is well-written, accurate, and free of errors.

- **Publish consistently:** Establish a regular publishing schedule to keep your readers engaged.

### Audience Engagement

- **Encourage comments and discussion:** Foster a sense of community by allowing readers to interact with your content and each other.

- **Respond to comments and feedback:** Show your readers that you value their input.

- **Run contests and giveaways:** Generate excitement and attract new readers.

### Analytics and Tracking

- **Track your website traffic:** Use tools like Google Analytics to understand your audience and how they interact with your website.

- **Monitor your social media engagement:** Track the performance of your social media posts and adjust your strategy accordingly.

- **Analyze your email marketing results:** Track open rates, click-through rates, and other metrics to measure the effectiveness of your email campaigns.

**Remember:** Building a successful blog or news website takes time and effort. Be patient, experiment with different strategies, and continuously learn and adapt to achieve your goals.

# 11.9 Conclusion

Building a thriving blog or news website requires a combination of high-quality content, effective promotion strategies, and a commitment to engaging your audience. By following the tips and best practices outlined in this chapter, you can create a platform that informs, inspires, and connects with readers, establishing your online presence as a valuable source of information and entertainment.

Remember, the key to success lies in consistently creating valuable content, actively promoting your website, and fostering a sense of community with your readers. As you continue your journey, embrace new technologies, adapt to changing trends, and always strive to provide the best possible experience for your audience. With dedication and passion, your blog or news website can become a powerful tool for sharing your voice and making a positive impact on the world.

***

# Chapter 12: Creating a Business Website

What will you learn:



## 12.1 Choosing the Right Theme for Your Business

The first step in creating a captivating business website is selecting the right theme. Think of your theme as the foundation and framework of your site's design and layout. Luckily, WordPress offers a vast array of both free and premium themes, each catering to different styles and functionalities. This abundance of options, however, can feel overwhelming for beginners. So, let's explore some key factors to consider when choosing the perfect theme for your business website:

- **Industry Relevance:** Start by browsing themes designed

specifically for your industry. Whether you're in e-commerce, photography, or professional services, industry-specific themes often come pre-loaded with features and functionalities that cater to your unique needs, saving you time and effort.

- **Design Aesthetics:** The visual appeal of your website is crucial for attracting and engaging visitors. Choose a theme that aligns with your brand identity and target audience. Consider elements like color schemes, typography, and overall style. Opt for a clean and uncluttered design that ensures easy navigation and readability.

- **Functionality:** Think about the features you want your website to have. Do you need an online store, a portfolio gallery, or a booking system? Many themes offer built-in functionalities or are compatible with popular plugins that extend your site's capabilities.

- **Responsiveness:** In today's mobile-driven world, your website must look and function flawlessly on all devices, from desktops to smartphones and tablets. Ensure the theme you choose is fully responsive, adapting seamlessly to different screen sizes.

## Popular Business Themes to Consider

To get you started, here are a few popular and versatile business themes known for their user-friendly interfaces and customization options:

- **Astra:** A lightweight and highly customizable theme with numerous pre-built website templates for various industries.

- **OceanWP** (Fig. 12.1): Another flexible theme offering extensive customization options and seamless integration with popular page builders.

- **GeneratePress:** Known for its speed and performance, GeneratePress is a clean and minimal theme ideal for building a variety of business websites.

- **Neve:** A fast and easily customizable theme with a focus on mobile-first design and compatibility with popular page builders.

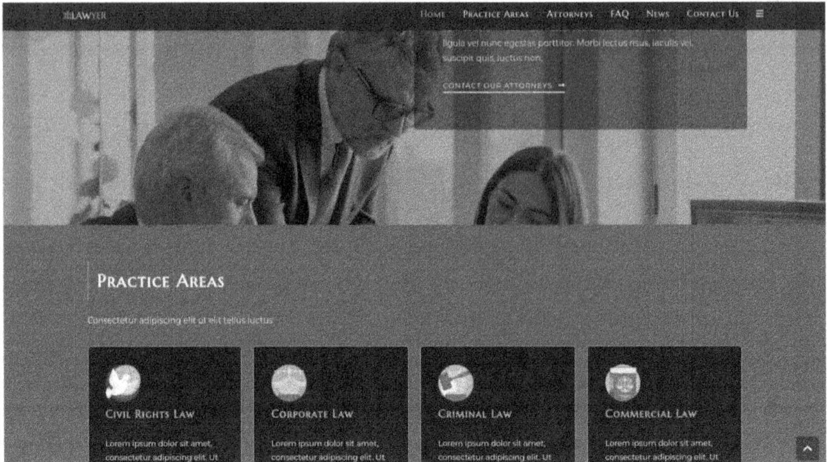


*Fig. 12.1 A Law Firm website demo provided by OceanWP Theme.*

Remember, selecting the right theme is a crucial first step, laying the groundwork for a stunning and functional business website. Take your time exploring the options, considering your specific needs and preferences, and don't hesitate to experiment until you find the perfect fit for your brand.

## 12.2 Essential Pages for Every Business Website

Every business website needs a core set of pages to effectively communicate with its audience and achieve its goals. These pages provide essential information, establish credibility, and guide visitors towards desired actions. Let's explore the must-have pages for your business website:

### 1. Homepage

- **The First Impression:** Your homepage is often the first point of contact with potential customers. It should create a captivating first impression and clearly communicate your brand identity, value proposition, and what sets you apart.

- **Clear and Compelling Headline:** Grab attention and succinctly convey what your business offers.

- **Engaging Visuals:** Use high-quality images or videos that represent your brand and resonate with your target audience.

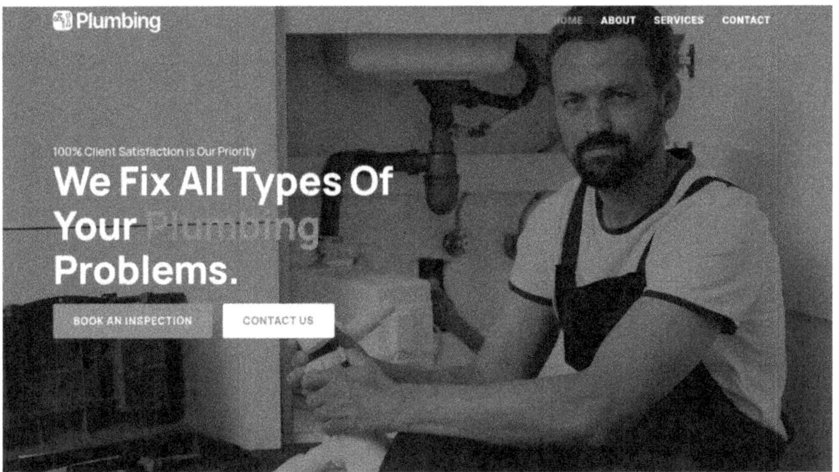


*Fig. 21.2 A Homepage of Plumbing business website demo provided by OceanWP Premium Theme.*

- **Concise and Informative Content:** Briefly explain what you do and the benefits you provide.

- **Call to Action:** Guide visitors towards the next step, whether it's exploring your products, contacting you, or signing up for a newsletter.

## 2. About Us

- **Tell Your Story:** Share your company's history, mission, values, and vision. Humanize your brand by introducing your team members and showcasing their expertise.

- **Building Trust:** The "About Us" page helps build trust and credibility with your audience. Share your achievements, awards, or testimonials to demonstrate your expertise and reliability.

## 3. Products/Services

- **Showcase Your Offerings:** Provide detailed descriptions of your products or services, highlighting their features, benefits, and value proposition.

- **High-Quality Visuals:** Include high-resolution images or videos that showcase your products from different angles and in use.

- **Clear Pricing:** If applicable, clearly display pricing information and any available options or variations.

- **Call to Action:** Encourage visitors to make a purchase, request a quote, or learn more.

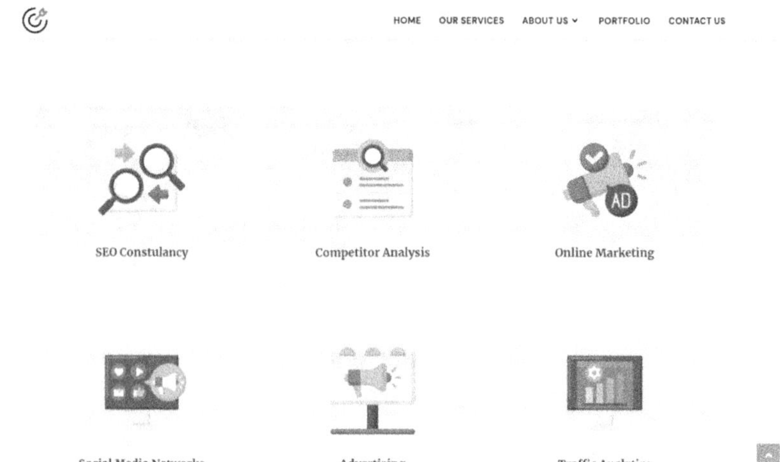


*Fig. 12.3 A service page demo of a digital marketing website provided by OceanWP Premium.*

## 4. Contact Us

- **Make it Easy to Connect:** Provide multiple ways for potential customers to reach you, such as a contact form, email address, phone number, and physical address (if applicable).

- **Consider a Map:** Embedding a Google Map makes it easy for visitors to locate your business.

- **Social Media Links:** Include links to your social media profiles to encourage further engagement.

## 5. Blog

- **Establish Thought Leadership:** Share valuable insights, industry trends, and informative articles related to your field.

- **Engage Your Audience:** Regularly publish blog posts to keep your website fresh and attract repeat visitors.

- **SEO Benefits:** A blog helps improve your website's search engine optimization (SEO) by providing fresh content and relevant keywords.

**Remember**, these essential pages are the foundation of your online presence. By crafting compelling content and optimizing the user experience, you can effectively engage your audience, build trust, and ultimately achieve your business goals.

# 12.3 Building Your Homepage

*ig. 12.4 The homepage of our digital marketing company.*

The homepage of your business website is prime digital real estate. It's the first impression you make on potential customers, and it needs to be impactful. An effective homepage should be clear, informative, and persuasive, guiding visitors towards taking a desired action. Here are some key elements to consider when building a homepage that converts:

## 1. Prioritize Clarity and Focus

- Your homepage shouldn't try to be everything to everyone.

Identify your target audience and tailor your message to their needs.

- Use concise and easy-to-understand language. Avoid industry jargon and technical terms that might confuse visitors.

## 2. Hero Section that Captivates

- The hero section is the top portion of your homepage, often featuring a banner image or video. It should be visually appealing and attention-grabbing.

- Incorporate a strong value proposition that clearly communicates what your business does and the benefits it offers.

## 3. Intuitive Navigation

- Make it easy for visitors to find the information they're looking for.

- Employ a clear and user-friendly navigation menu that allows users to explore different sections of your website effortlessly.

## 4. Calls to Action (CTAs):

- Tell visitors what you want them to do next, whether it's contacting you, subscribing to a newsletter, or browsing your products.

- Use strong CTA buttons that are visually distinct and strategically placed throughout the homepage.

## 5. Social Proof and Credibility

- Showcase positive customer testimonials, client logos, or industry awards to build trust and establish credibility.

- Feature statistics or data that highlight your achievements and the value you provide.

## 6. Mobile-Friendly Design

- Ensure your homepage is optimized for viewing on all devices, especially smartphones and tablets.

- A responsive design that adapts to different screen sizes will provide a seamless user experience for all visitors.

By following these guidelines, create a homepage that effectively captures attention, conveys your brand message, and compels visitors to take action. Remember, your homepage is a dynamic space, so keep testing and refining it to optimize its performance.

# 12.4 Adding Products or Services

Showcasing your products or services effectively is crucial for any business website. WordPress offers several methods to achieve this, from utilizing Gutenberg blocks to dedicated eCommerce plugins. Let's explore the options:

## Using Gutenberg Blocks for Simple Product/Service Display

- **Gutenberg Blocks:** For basic product or service listings, you can utilize various Gutenberg blocks:

  - **Image Block:** Showcase product images with the Image block.

  - **Gallery Block:** Create image galleries for products with multiple visuals.

  - **Heading and Paragraph Blocks:** Provide product or service names, descriptions, and key features.

  - **List Block:** Highlight key features or specifications in a bulleted or numbered list.

  - **Button Block:** Add a call to action button for inquiries or purchases.

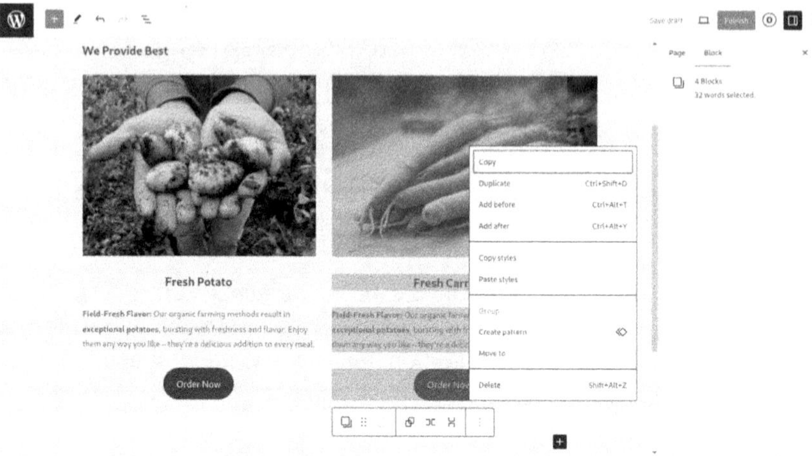

Fig. *2.5 Designing a product section using Gutenberg block*

- **Columns Block:** Organize your products or services into columns for a visually appealing layout.

- **Group Block:** Combine multiple blocks into a group to easily manage and style them together.

# WooCommerce: A Powerful eCommerce Solution

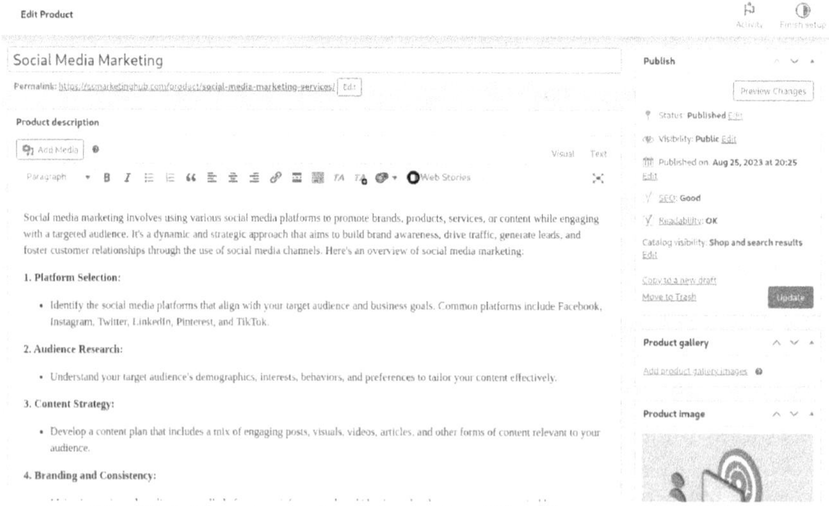

*Fig.12.6 Creating a Product using WooCommerce plugin.*

- **Dedicated eCommerce Plugin:** WooCommerce is a popular and free plugin that transforms your WordPress website into a fully functional online store.

- **Product Management:** Easily add and manage products, including variations, attributes, inventory, and shipping options.

- **Payment Gateways:** Integrate with various payment gateways to accept secure online payments.

- **Order Management:** Track and manage customer orders, shipping, and inventory with ease.

- **Additional Features:** Extend WooCommerce's functionality with numerous extensions for marketing, subscriptions, memberships, and more.

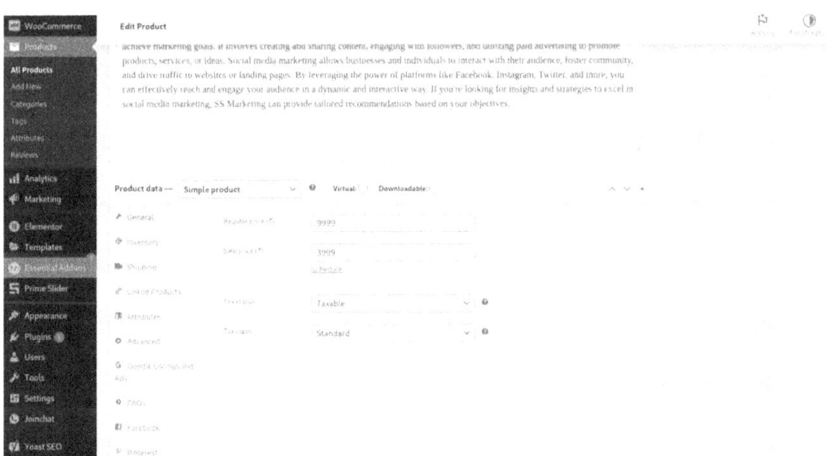

*Fig. 12.7 Editing a simple product in WooCommerce plugin*

## Creating Product/Service Pages

- **Gutenberg or WooCommerce:** Choose your preferred method based on your needs. For simple listings, Gutenberg blocks might suffice. For a full-fledged online store, WooCommerce is recommended, we will learn deep in next Chapter.

- **Product Information:** Provide detailed and accurate product descriptions, including features, benefits, specifications, and high-quality images or videos.

- **Product Variations:** If applicable, showcase different product options, such as sizes, colors, or materials, using variation functionality.

- **Pricing and Availability:** Clearly display pricing information and indicate product availability.

- **Call to Action:** Include a prominent call to action button to guide customers towards purchasing or inquiring about the product/service.

## Additional Considerations

- **Product Categories and Tags:** Organize your products or services into categories and use tags for easier navigation and search functionality.

- **Product Reviews and Ratings**: Encourage customer reviews and ratings to build trust and social proof.

- **Shipping and Returns:** Clearly communicate your shipping and return policies to manage customer expectations.

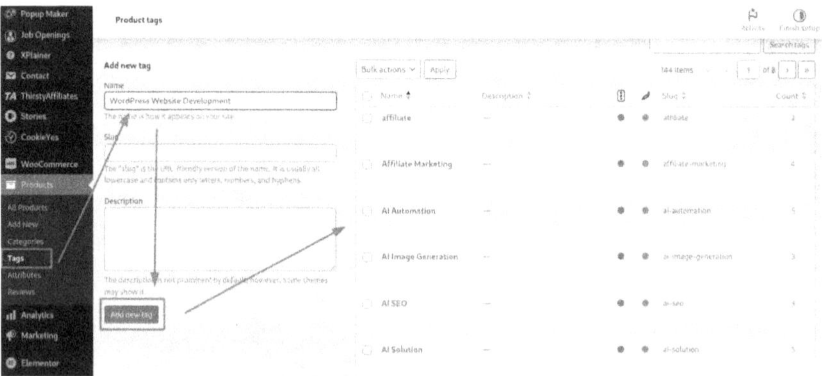

Fig. 12.8 Creating a tag for products in the WooCommerce plugin.

Whether you choose Gutenberg or a dedicated eCommerce plugin like WooCommerce, effectively showcasing your products or services is crucial for driving sales and growing your business online. I recommend you to wait till  the next chapter for more knowledge about eCommerce websites.

## 12.5 Showcasing Testimonials and Case Studies

Testimonials and case studies are powerful tools for building trust and credibility with potential customers. They provide social proof and demonstrate the real-world value and effectiveness of your products or services. Let's explore how to showcase them effectively on your website:

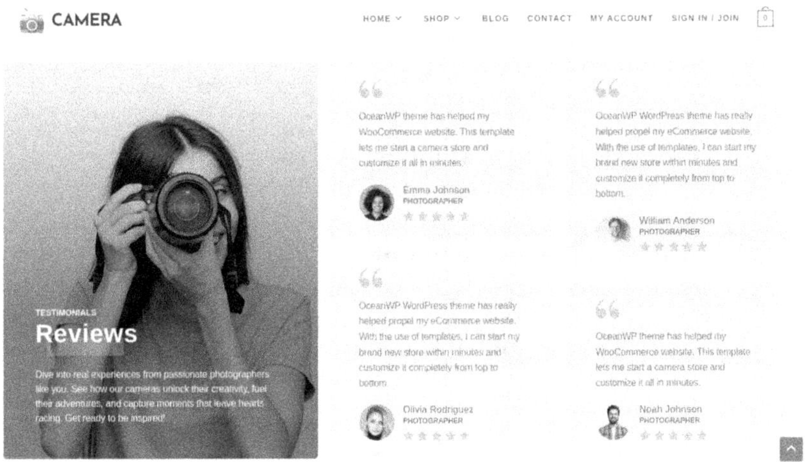


*Fig. 12.8 A testimonial section demo from OceanWP Premium theme.*

### The Importance of Social Proof

- **Building Trust:** Testimonials and case studies offer unbiased opinions and experiences from past customers, which helps build trust and credibility with potential buyers.

- **Demonstrating Value:** They showcase the positive impact of your products or services, highlighting the benefits and results achieved by others.

- **Overcoming Objections:** Testimonials can address common customer concerns and objections, providing reassurance and encouraging conversions.

# Ways to Showcase Testimonials

- **Gutenberg Blocks:**

    - **Quote Block:** Use the Quote block to display testimonials with attribution to the source.

    - **Image Block:** Include headshots of the individuals providing the testimonials to add a personal touch.

    - **Columns Block:** Arrange multiple testimonials side-by-side for a visually appealing layout.

- **Testimonial Plugins:** Several plugins offer dedicated features for showcasing testimonials, such as:

    - **Testimonial Rotator:** Create slideshows or grids of testimonials that automatically rotate.

    - **Testimonial Submission Forms:** Allow customers to easily submit testimonials directly on your website.

    - **Styling and Customization:** Choose from various layouts, themes, and styles to match your website's design.

# Case Studies

- **Detailed Stories:** Case studies provide in-depth narratives of how your products or services have helped specific clients achieve their goals.

- **Data and Metrics:** Include quantifiable results and data to demonstrate the impact of your offerings.

- **Problem-Solution Format:** Structure your case studies by outlining the client's challenge, your solution, and the positive outcomes achieved.

- **Visuals and Storytelling:** Utilize visuals like charts, graphs, and images to enhance your storytelling and make the case study more engaging.

## Placement and Integration

- **Homepage:** Feature key testimonials on your homepage to make a strong first impression.

- **Product/Service Pages:** Include relevant testimonials and case studies on specific product or service pages to highlight their effectiveness.

- **Dedicated Testimonial Page:** Create a dedicated page showcasing a collection of testimonials and case studies.

- **Blog Posts:** Integrate testimonials and case studies into blog content to support your claims and add credibility.

**Remember,** showcasing testimonials and case studies effectively can significantly impact your website's ability to convert visitors into customers. By leveraging the power of social proof, you can build trust, demonstrate value, and ultimately achieve your business goals.

# 12.6 Integrating Contact Forms and Maps

Providing easy ways for potential customers to contact you is crucial for generating leads and building relationships. Let's explore two essential elements for facilitating communication on your  website: contact forms and maps.

## Contact Forms

- **Why Contact Forms?** Contact forms offer several advantages over simply displaying an email address:

- **Spam Reduction:** They help reduce spam by avoiding the exposure of your email address to bots and scrapers.

- **Organized Data Collection:** They allow you to collect specific information from inquiries, such as name, email address, phone number, and the nature of the inquiry.

- **Professionalism:** Contact forms present a more professional image and streamlined communication process.

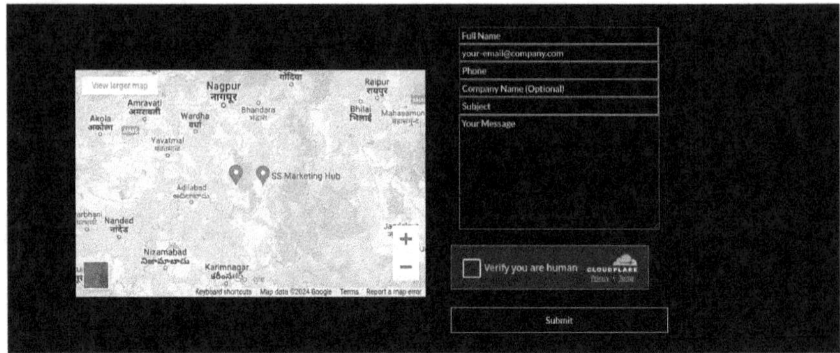



*Fig. 12.9 A map and a contact form from our company contact page.*

## Popular Contact Form Plugins

- **Contact Form 7:** A widely used and free plugin offering basic contact form functionality with customizable fields and email notifications.

- **WPForms:** A user-friendly plugin with a drag-and-drop interface, pre-built form templates, and advanced features like conditional logic and file uploads.

- **Gravity Forms:** A premium plugin offering powerful features like multi-page forms, user registration, payment integrations, and advanced conditional logic.

## Creating and Customizing Contact Forms

1. **Choose a Plugin:** Select a contact form plugin that suits your needs and budget.

2. **Create a New Form:** Most plugins offer a form builder interface where you can add and customize fields.

3. **Essential Fields:** Include essential fields like name, email address, and a message box. You can also add optional fields specific to your requirements, such as phone number or subject line.

4. **Form Settings:** Configure email notifications to receive alerts when someone submits a form. You can also customize the

confirmation message displayed after submission.

5. **Embed the Form:** Use the provided shortcode or block to embed the contact form on your desired page, typically the "Contact Us" page.

## Integrating Maps

- **Visual Representation:** Embedding a map on your website visually showcases your business location and helps potential customers find you easily.

- **Google Maps Integration:** Google Maps is the most popular mapping platform and integrates seamlessly with WordPress.

*ig. 12.10 Creating a form in the 'Contact Form 7' plugin.*

## Embedding a Google Map

1. **Obtain the Embed Code:** Go to Google Maps and search for your business location. Click the "Share" button and select "Embed a map." Copy the provided HTML code.

2. **Embed in WordPress:** You can embed the code directly into a "Custom HTML" block in Gutenberg or use a dedicated Google Maps plugin for additional features like customizable markers and styling options.

## Additional Considerations

- **Contact Page Content:** Provide additional contact information on your "Contact Us" page, such as phone number, email address, social media links, and business hours.

- **Call to Action:** Encourage visitors to contact you with a clear call to action, such as "Get in Touch" or "Request a Quote."

- **Responsiveness:** Ensure your contact form and map display correctly on all devices.

By integrating contact forms and maps into your website, you provide convenient and accessible ways for potential customers to connect with your business, fostering communication and driving potential leads.

# 12.7 Search Engine Optimization (SEO) Basics

*Fig. 12.11 Managing SEO of a page using the 'Yoast SEO' plugin.*

Search Engine Optimization (SEO) is the practice of improving your website's visibility in search engine results pages (SERPs) like Google. By optimizing your website for relevant keywords and following SEO best practices, you can attract more organic traffic and reach a wider audience.

# Key SEO Principles

- **Keyword Research:** Identify relevant keywords and phrases that your target audience is searching for. Use keyword research tools like Google Keyword Planner or SEMrush to discover search volume and competition levels.

- **On-Page Optimization:** Optimize your website content and HTML source code to align with target keywords. This includes:

  - **Title Tags:** Write clear and concise title tags that accurately reflect the page content and include relevant keywords.

  - **Meta Descriptions:** Craft compelling meta descriptions that entice users to click on your website in search results.

  - **Headings:** Structure your content with headings (H1, H2, H3) that incorporate keywords and guide readers through the text.

  - **Image Alt Text:** Describe images using relevant keywords in the "alt text" attribute, which helps search engines understand the image content.

  - **Internal Linking:** Link to other relevant pages within your website to improve navigation and distribute SEO value.

# SEO Plugins for WordPress

- **Yoast SEO:** A popular and comprehensive plugin that offers on-page optimization analysis, keyword suggestions, XML sitemap generation, and readability checks.

- **Rank Math:** Another powerful SEO plugin with features similar to Yoast SEO, along with additional functionalities like schema markup, local SEO tools, and keyword rank tracking.

# Additional SEO Considerations

- **Content Quality:** Create high-quality, informative, and engaging content that provides value to your audience.

- **Mobile-Friendliness:** Ensure your website is responsive and optimized for mobile devices, as Google prioritizes mobile-friendly websites in search results.

- **Website Speed:** Improve your website's loading speed, as it affects both user experience and search engine rankings.

- **Backlinks:** Earn backlinks from other reputable websites to increase your website's authority and credibility in the eyes of search engines.

SEO is an ongoing process that requires consistent effort and adaptation to search engine algorithms. By understanding the basic principles and utilizing available tools, you can improve your website's visibility in search results and attract more organic traffic to your business.

# 12.8 Connecting Social Media

Social media platforms offer powerful channels for connecting with your audience, building brand awareness, and driving traffic to your website. Integrating social media into your business website creates a cohesive online presence and encourages engagement.

## Benefits of Social Media Integration

- **Increased Reach and Visibility:** Share your website content on social media to reach a wider audience and attract new visitors.

- **Enhanced Engagement:** Encourage social interactions and discussions around your brand and content.

- **Social Proof and Credibility:** Showcase social media activity and follower counts on your website to build trust and credibility.

- **Traffic Generation:** Drive traffic from social media platforms back to your website, increasing the potential for conversions.

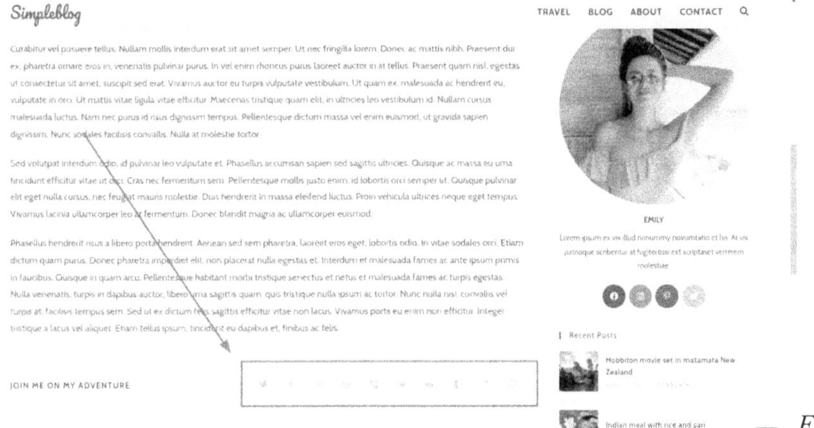

*ig. 12.12 A social media share buttons section on blog demo by the OceanWP Premium theme.*

# Ways to Connect Social Media with Your Website

- **Social Media Buttons:** Add social media buttons to your website, making it easy for visitors to share your content and follow your profiles. Place buttons strategically on your homepage, blog posts, and product pages.

- **Social Media Feeds:** Embed social media feeds directly on your website to showcase your latest posts and activity. This keeps your website content fresh and encourages visitors to engage with your social media channels.

- **Social Login:** Allow users to log in to your website using their social media credentials for a more convenient and streamlined experience.

- **Social Sharing Plugins:** Utilize plugins that offer additional social sharing features, such as share counts, customized button styles, and social media analytics.

# Popular Social Media Plugins for WordPress

- **Social Media Share Buttons & Social Sharing Icons:** Offers a wide range of customizable social media buttons and sharing options.

- **Smash Balloon Social Photo Feed:** Allows you to easily display Instagram feeds on your website with various customization options.

- **Social Login & Register:** Enables social login and registration functionalities using various social media platforms.

## Additional Considerations

- **Choose Relevant Platforms:** Focus on the social media platforms where your target audience is most active.

- **Consistent Branding:** Maintain consistent branding across your website and social media profiles for a cohesive online presence.

- **Engagement Strategy:** Develop a social media engagement strategy to actively interact with your audience and foster community building.

- **Track and Analyze:** Monitor your social media performance and website traffic to measure the impact of your integration efforts.

By effectively connecting your social media and website, you create a more engaging online presence, expand your reach, and drive valuable traffic to your business.

# 12.9 Analyzing Website Traffic with Google Analytics

Understanding how users interact with your website is crucial for optimizing its performance and achieving your business goals. Google Analytics is a powerful and free tool that provides valuable insights into your website traffic and user behavior.

## What is Google Analytics?

- **Website Traffic Analysis:** Google Analytics tracks and reports on various website metrics, including:

- **Number of Visitors:** Total number of users who visited your website within a specific timeframe.

- **Page Views:** The number of times individual pages on your website were viewed.

- **Unique Visitors:** The number of individual users who visited your website, excluding repeat visits from the same user.

- **Bounce Rate:** The percentage of visitors who leave your website after viewing only one page.

- **Average Session Duration:** The average amount of time users spend on your website per visit.

- **Traffic Sources:** Identify where your website traffic originates from, such as organic search, social media, paid advertising, or referral links.

## Benefits of Using Google Analytics

- **Performance Measurement:** Track key website metrics to measure the effectiveness of your SEO, marketing campaigns, and content strategies.

- **User Behavior Insights:** Understand how users navigate your website, which pages they visit, and how long they stay. This information helps identify areas for improvement and optimize the user experience.

- **Goal Tracking:** Set up goals to track conversions, such as form submissions, product purchases, or newsletter signups.

- **Data-Driven Decision Making:** Use data from Google Analytics to make informed decisions about your website content, design, and marketing efforts.

## Getting Started with Google Analytics

1. Install Site Kit by Google plugin.

2. Connect your Gmail account.

3.  Site Kit automatically adds tracking code (no coding needed).

4.  View basic metrics in your WordPress dashboard.

## Key Metrics to Monitor

- **Overall Traffic Trends:** Monitor overall website traffic growth and identify any significant spikes or dips.

- **Top Traffic Sources:** Analyze which channels are driving the most traffic to your website and focus your efforts on those channels.

- **User Engagement:** Track metrics like bounce rate, average session duration, and pages per session to gauge user engagement with your website content.

- **Goal Conversions:** Monitor your goal completion rates to measure the effectiveness of your marketing campaigns and website optimization efforts.

By regularly analyzing website traffic with Google Analytics, you gain valuable insights into user behavior and website performance. This data empowers you to make data-driven decisions, optimize your website, and ultimately achieve your business goals.

# 12.10 Essential Plugins for Business Websites

WordPress plugins extend the functionality of your website, offering a vast array of features and tools to enhance its capabilities. Let's explore some essential plugins that can benefit your business website:

## SEO Plugins

**Yoast SEO or Rank Math:** As I mentioned earlier, these plugins offer comprehensive on-page optimization analysis, keyword suggestions, XML sitemap generation, and other SEO tools to improve your website's search engine visibility.

## Security Plugins

- **Wordfence Security:** A popular security plugin that provides firewall protection, malware scanning, login security features, and security incident alerts.

- **Sucuri:** Offers website security solutions like malware removal, website firewall, DDoS protection, and security monitoring.

## Performance Plugins

- **WP Super Cache:** A caching plugin that improves website speed by creating static HTML files of your pages, reducing server load times.

- **W3 Total Cache:** Another popular caching plugin with advanced features for optimizing website performance.

- **Smush:** Optimizes images by compressing file sizes without compromising quality, leading to faster page loading times.

## Marketing Automation Plugins

- **Mailchimp for WordPress:** Integrates your website with Mailchimp, allowing you to collect email addresses, manage subscribers, and create email marketing campaigns.

- **OptinMonster:** A powerful lead generation plugin that helps you create opt-in forms, popups, and other tools to convert website visitors into subscribers or customers.

## Other Useful Plugins

- **Contact Form 7 or WPForms:** As discussed earlier, these plugins facilitate easy creation and management of contact forms.

- **Akismet Anti-Spam:** Protects your website from spam comments and form submissions.

- **UpdraftPlus:** A reliable backup plugin that allows you to schedule automatic backups of your website files and database.

- **MonsterInsights:** Provides insights into your website traffic and user behavior directly within your WordPress dashboard, using data from Google Analytics.

By utilizing essential plugins, you can enhance your business website's functionality, improve security and performance, and achieve your marketing goals more effectively.

# 12.11 Maintaining and Updating Your Website

A successful business website requires ongoing maintenance and regular updates to ensure optimal performance, security, and functionality. Neglecting updates can lead to vulnerabilities, compatibility issues, and a decline in user experience.

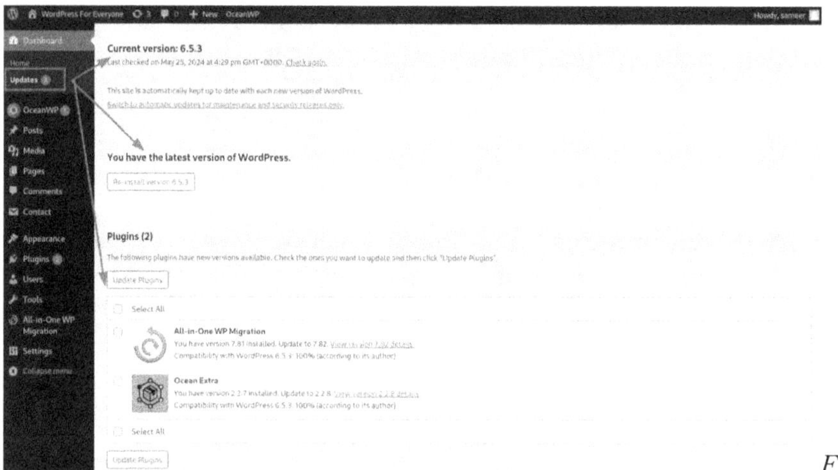

*ig. 12.13 Maintaining updates of a WordPress website.*

## Importance of Regular Updates

- **Security:** Updates often include security patches that address vulnerabilities and protect your website from hackers and malware.

- **Compatibility:** Updates ensure compatibility with the latest versions of WordPress, themes, and plugins, preventing conflicts and errors.

- **Functionality:** Updates may introduce new features, improvements, and bug fixes that enhance your website's functionality and user experience.

- **Performance:** Updates can optimize website speed and performance, leading to a better user experience and improved search engine rankings.

## What to Update?

1. **WordPress Core:** The core WordPress software should be updated to the latest version whenever a new release is available.

2. **Themes:** Update your WordPress theme regularly to benefit from new features, bug fixes, and security enhancements.

3. **Plugins:** Keep your plugins updated to ensure compatibility with the latest version of WordPress and address any security vulnerabilities.

## Performing Updates Safely

- **Backup Your Website:** Always create a complete backup of your website before performing any updates. This ensures you can restore your website in case of any issues during the update process.

- **Update One at a Time:** Update plugins and themes individually to identify any potential conflicts or errors.

- **Test After Updates:** After updating, thoroughly test your website to ensure everything is functioning correctly.

## Maintenance Tasks

- **Regular Backups:** Schedule regular backups of your website to protect against data loss due to technical issues, hacking attempts, or accidental deletions.

- **Security Monitoring:** Implement security measures like strong passwords, two-factor authentication, and security plugins to monitor and protect your website from threats.

- **Performance Optimization:** Regularly monitor your website's speed and performance and take necessary steps to optimize loading times.

- **Content Updates:** Keep your website content fresh and relevant by regularly adding new blog posts, updating product information, and reviewing existing content for accuracy.

By establishing a routine maintenance schedule and keeping your website up-to-date, you ensure its security, functionality, and performance, creating a positive user experience and supporting your business goals.

## 12.12 Conclusion

Building a business website with WordPress opens doors to countless possibilities. Throughout this chapter, we've explored the essential elements of creating a functional and engaging website, from choosing the right theme and crafting essential pages to showcasing your products or services and optimizing for search engines. Remember, your website is a dynamic platform that evolves alongside your business. As you grow and your goals change, so too will your website's needs.

Continue to explore, experiment, and refine your website to ensure it effectively represents your brand, connects with your audience, and drives desired results. Whether you're just starting out or looking to expand your online presence, WordPress empowers you to create a website that reflects your unique vision and supports your business journey.

***

# Chapter 13: Creating an Online Store

What will you learn:



## 13.1 Introduction

The rise of e-commerce has revolutionized the way we shop and do business. With WordPress, you can easily transform your website into a powerful online store, allowing you to sell products or services to a global audience. Whether you're a small business owner, an entrepreneur, or an established brand, creating an online store opens up new opportunities for growth and success.

In this chapter, we'll explore the essential steps involved in building and managing an online store using WordPress. We'll begin by discussing the importance of choosing the right e-commerce plugin and guide you through the process of setting up your store. Then, we'll delve into adding and managing products, configuring payment gateways and shipping options, and ensuring the security and legal compliance of your online store.

We'll also explore effective marketing and promotion strategies to attract customers and drive sales. Finally, we'll share valuable tips and best practices to help you create a successful online store that delivers a seamless shopping experience for your customers.

Get ready to embark on your e-commerce journey and unlock the potential of online selling!

*Fig. 13.1 An ecommerce website demo by OceanWP Premium theme.*

## 13.2 Choosing an E-commerce Plugin

WordPress, a powerful content management system, can be transformed into a full-fledged online store with the help of e-commerce plugins. Here's a breakdown of some major players in this arena:

- **WooCommerce:** The undisputed king of WordPress e-commerce, WooCommerce boasts a massive user base and a reputation for ease of use. Completely free to download, it offers a user-friendly interface, extensive product management features, and a shopping cart system. Its true strength lies in its vast ecosystem of extensions, allowing you to add functionalities like payment gateways, shipping options, marketing tools, and more (often at an additional cost). However, managing a large number of extensions can impact website performance.

- **Easy Digital Downloads (EDD):** This plugin shines when it comes to selling digital products like ebooks, software, or online courses. Lightweight and focused, EDD streamlines the sales process for downloadable items. It integrates seamlessly with WordPress and offers core functionalities like discount codes, customer management, and download delivery. While EDD can be extended with add-ons, it may not be suitable for stores selling physical products due to a lack of advanced inventory management and shipping features.

- **BigCommerce for WordPress:** This offering from a leading e-commerce platform brings BigCommerce's robust features directly to your WordPress site. It boasts a user-friendly interface, powerful product management tools, built-in marketing functionalities, and a wide range of payment gateways. BigCommerce for WordPress offers a free plan with limited features, but unlocking its full potential requires a paid subscription. While feature-rich, it might have a steeper learning curve compared to some free options.

- **Ecwid Ecommerce Shopping Cart:** Known for its ease of use and affordability, Ecwid offers a free plan with basic functionalities to get you started. It integrates seamlessly with your WordPress site and allows you to sell across multiple platforms like Facebook and Instagram. However, the free plan has limitations on product quantity and bandwidth. Upgrading unlocks advanced features like product variants, abandoned cart recovery, and real-time shipping rates, but comes at a cost.

- **WP EasyCart:** This user-friendly plugin caters to businesses with simpler needs. It offers a clean interface for product management, shopping cart functionality, and basic marketing tools. WP EasyCart integrates with popular payment gateways and email marketing services. It has a free plan with limited features, while premium versions offer advanced functionalities like product subscriptions and discount codes.

## Factors to Consider When Choosing a Plugin

- **Features:** Evaluate the features offered by each plugin and ensure they align with your specific needs, such as product types, payment gateways, and shipping options.

- **Ease of Use:** Choose a plugin with a user-friendly interface that is easy to navigate and manage.

- **Customization Options:** Consider the level of customization available, allowing you to tailor the look and feel of your online store

- **Cost:** Some plugins are free, while others offer premium versions with additional features.

- **Support:** Choose a plugin with a strong support community and reliable documentation.

## Recommendation

For most beginners and small businesses, **WooCommerce** is a great starting point due to its extensive features, ease of use, and large community.

**Remember:** Choosing the right e-commerce plugin is crucial for the success of your online store. Carefully evaluate your needs and research different options before making a decision.

# 13.3 Setting Up Your Online Store

Once you've chosen your e-commerce plugin, it's time to set up your online store. Here's a general overview of the steps involved:

## Install and Activate the Plugin

1. Go to "Plugins" > "Add New" in your WordPress dashboard.

2. Search for your chosen e-commerce plugin and click "Install Now".

3. Once the plugin is installed, click "Activate".

## Configure Basic Settings

Most ecommerce plugins will guide you through a setup wizard to configure basic settings such as:

- **Store Location:** Set your country, state, and currency.

- **Shipping and Tax:** Configure shipping zones and tax rates.

- **Payment Gateways:** Choose the payment methods you want to accept (e.g., PayPal, Stripe).

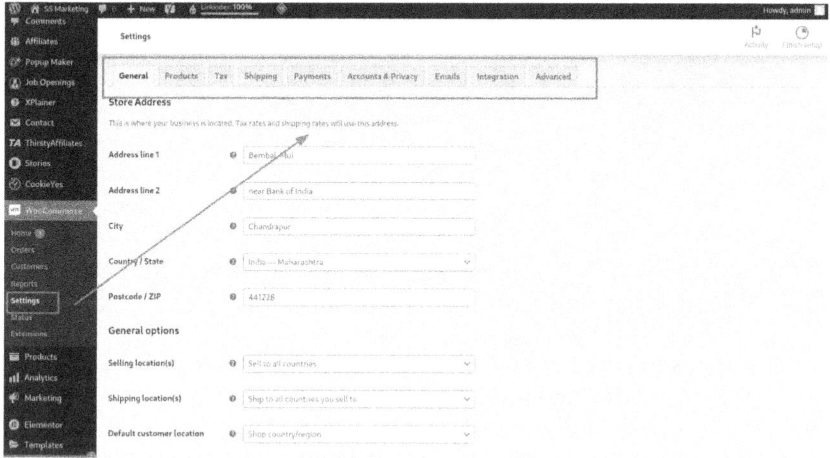

*Fig. 13.2 The settings of the WooCommerce plugin.*

## Customize Your Store Design

- Choose a theme that is compatible with your e-commerce plugin or customize your existing theme to integrate seamlessly with your online store.

- Customize the appearance of your product pages, shopping cart, and checkout process.

## Add Pages

Create essential pages for your online store, such as:

- **Shop Page:** This is where your products will be displayed.

- **Cart Page:** This page allows customers to view and manage their shopping cart.

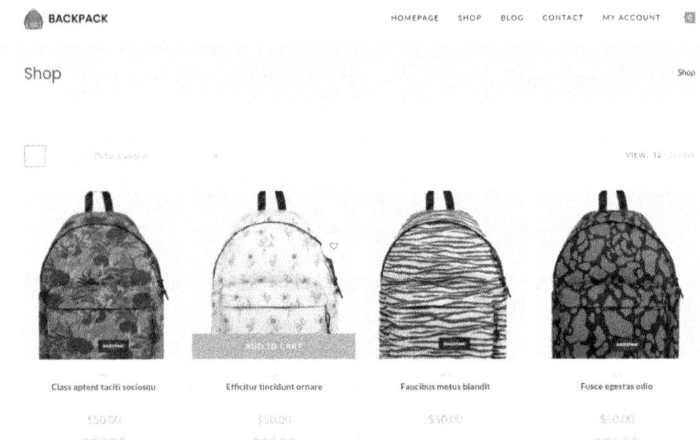



*Fig. 13.3 A shop page demo by OceanWP Premium theme.*

- **Checkout Page:** This page allows customers to enter their shipping and payment information and complete their purchase.

- **My Account Page:** This page allows customers to manage their account information and order history.

**Note**: Some ecommerce plugins automatically create these pages, you don't need to recreate them.

## Test Your Store

Before launching your online store, thoroughly test all functionalities, including adding products to the cart, going through the checkout process, and processing payments.

## Additional Considerations

- **Legal Pages:** Create pages for your privacy policy, terms and conditions, and return policy.

- **Security:** Implement security measures to protect your website and customer data.

- **SEO:** Optimize your product pages and other content for search engines.

By following these steps, you can set up a functional and visually appealing online store that is ready to welcome customers.

# 13.4 Adding and Managing Products

The heart of your online store lies in your products. Here's how to add and manage products effectively:

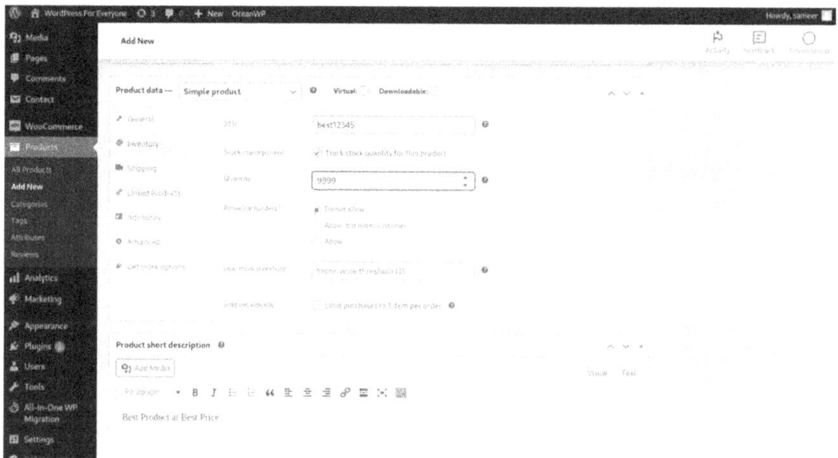

Fig. 13.4 Adding a new product using WooCommerce plugin.

## Adding New Products

1.  Go to the "Products" section in your WordPress dashboard.

2.  Click "Add New" to create a new product.

## Enter the product details

- **Product Name:** A clear and descriptive name for your product.

- **Product Description:** A detailed description of the product, including features, benefits, and specifications.

- **Product Images:** Upload high-quality images of your product from different angles.

- **Price:** Set the price of your product.

- **Inventory:** Specify the quantity of the product in stock.

- **Shipping Options:** Configure shipping options for the product, such as weight and dimensions.

- **Product Categories and Tags:** Assign categories and tags to your product for better organization and searchability.

## Product Types

1. **Simple Products:** Physical or digital products with a single variation.

2. **Variable Products:** Products with multiple variations, such as size, color, or material.

3. **Grouped Products:** A collection of related products that can be purchased together.

4. **External/Affiliate Products**: Products that are listed on your website but sold on another platform.

## Managing Products

- **Edit existing products:** Update product information, pricing, or inventory as needed.

- **Track inventory:** Monitor your stock levels and update them regularly.

- **Manage orders:** Process orders, update order status, and communicate with customers.

## Additional Considerations

- **Product Variations:** For variable products, create different variations with unique SKUs, prices, and inventory levels.

- **Product Images:** Use high-quality images that showcase your products in the best light.

- **Product Descriptions:** Write clear and compelling descriptions that highlight the benefits of your products.

- **Product Categories and Tags:** Organize your products effectively for easy browsing and search.

By effectively adding and managing your products, you can create a well-organized and user-friendly online store that showcases your offerings and drives sales.

# 13.5 Payment Gateways and Shipping Options

To complete transactions and deliver products to customers, you need to configure payment gateways and shipping options in your online store.

## Payment Gateways

1. **Choose a payment gateway:** Popular options include PayPal, PayU, Razorpay, Stripe, Square, and Authorize.net. Consider transaction fees, supported currencies, and ease of integration with your e-commerce plugin.

2. **Configure your payment gateway:** Follow the instructions provided by your chosen gateway to connect it to your online store.

3. **Test your payment gateway:** Ensure that payments are processed smoothly before launching your store.

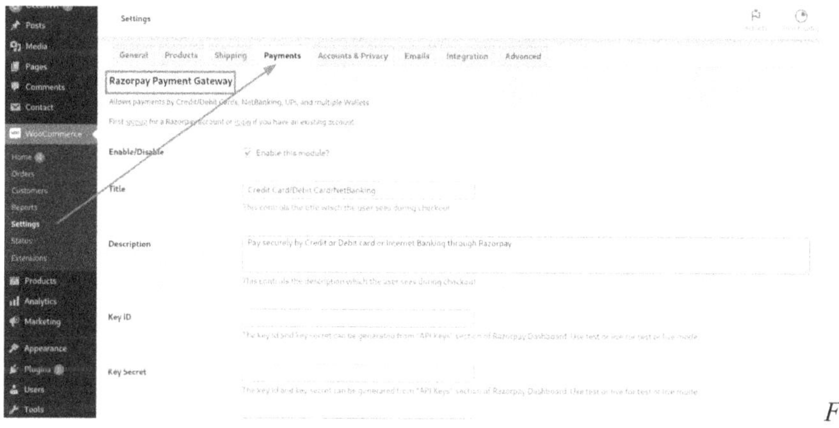

*ig. 13.5 Configuring Razorpay Payment Gateway to WooCommerce.*

## Shipping Options

- **Set up shipping zones:** Define different shipping zones based on geographic location.

- **Configure shipping methods:** Offer various shipping methods, such as flat rate, free shipping, or real-time carrier rates.

- **Set shipping rates:** Determine shipping costs based on factors like weight, dimensions, destination, and shipping method.

- **Offer local pickup:** If applicable, provide an option for customers to pick up their orders in person.

## Additional Considerations

- **Taxes:** Configure tax rates based on your location and applicable laws.

- **Shipping labels:** Consider using a service that allows you to print shipping labels directly from your WordPress dashboard.

- **Shipping insurance:** Offer shipping insurance to protect against lost or damaged packages.

## Tips for Choosing Payment Gateways and Shipping Options

- **Consider your target audience:** Choose payment gateways and shipping options that are popular in your target market.

- **Keep it simple:** Offer a manageable number of payment and shipping options to avoid overwhelming customers.

- **Be transparent about costs:** Clearly display shipping costs and any applicable taxes during the checkout process.

By providing convenient and reliable payment and shipping options, you can create a positive shopping experience for your customers and increase sales.

# 13.6 Security and Legal Considerations

Running an online store comes with responsibilities for ensuring security and legal compliance. Here are some key considerations:

## Security

- **Secure your website:** Implement security measures to protect your website from hackers and malware. This includes using strong passwords, keeping your software updated, and using a security plugin.

- **Use a secure hosting provider:** Choose a hosting provider that offers robust security features, such as firewalls and malware scanning.

- **Protect customer data:** Ensure that customer data, including payment information, is securely stored and transmitted. Use SSL certificates to encrypt data transmission.

- **PCI Compliance:** If you process credit card payments directly on your website, ensure you comply with Payment Card Industry Data Security Standards (PCI DSS).

## Legal Considerations

- **Terms and Conditions:** Create clear terms and conditions that outline the rules and regulations for using your online store.

- **Privacy Policy:** Inform customers how you collect, use, and protect their personal information.

- **Return Policy:** Establish a clear return policy that outlines the process for returning or exchanging products.

- **Shipping Policy:** Clearly communicate your shipping policies, including shipping costs, delivery times, and international shipping options.

- **Taxes:** Understand and comply with applicable tax laws in your region and for any regions you ship to.

## Additional Considerations

- **Accessibility:** Ensure your online store is accessible to users with disabilities.

- **Data Protection:** Comply with data protection regulations such as GDPR (General Data Protection Regulation) or CCPA (California Consumer Privacy Act).

**Remember:** Security and legal compliance are essential for building trust with your customers and protecting your business. Consult with legal and security professionals to ensure your online store meets all necessary requirements.

## 13.7 Marketing and Promoting Your Online Store

Once your online store is up and running, it's time to attract customers and drive sales. Here are some effective marketing and promotion strategies:

### Search Engine Optimization (SEO)

- **Optimize your product pages:** Use relevant keywords in product titles, descriptions, and meta tags.

- **Build backlinks:** Get other websites to link to your product pages.

- **Create high-quality content:** Publish blog posts, articles, and other content that is relevant to your target audience and includes links to your products.

### Social Media Marketing

- **Promote your products on social media:** Share product images, videos, and special offers on platforms like Facebook, Instagram, and Pinterest.

- **Run social media ads:** Target your ideal customers with paid advertising campaigns.

- **Engage with your followers:** Respond to comments, answer questions, and build relationships with potential customers.

## Email Marketing

- **Build an email list:** Offer incentives for customers to subscribe to your email list.

- **Send promotional emails:** Share new products, special offers, and exclusive discounts with your subscribers.

- **Personalize your emails:** Segment your audience and send targeted emails based on their interests and purchase history.

## Content Marketing

- **Create valuable content:** Publish blog posts, articles, and videos that educate and inform your target audience about your products and industry.

- **Guest blogging:** Write guest posts for other websites in your niche to reach a new audience.

- **Influencer marketing:** Partner with influencers in your industry to promote your products.

## Paid Advertising

- **Google Ads:** Run pay-per-click (PPC) ads to target specific keywords and drive traffic to your product pages.

- **Social media advertising:** Use paid advertising options on platforms like Facebook and Instagram to reach a wider audience.

## Other Marketing Strategies

- **Affiliate marketing:** Partner with other businesses to promote your products in exchange for a commission.

- **Loyalty programs:** Reward repeat customers with discounts and exclusive offers.

- **Customer reviews:** Encourage customers to leave reviews on your website and other platforms.

**Remember:** Marketing your online store is an ongoing process. Experiment with different strategies, track your results, and adjust your approach as needed to reach your target audience and achieve your sales goals.

## 13.8 Tips and Best Practices

Here are some additional tips and best practices to help you create a successful online store:

### Product Presentation

- **High-quality images:** Use professional-looking product images that showcase your products in the best light.

- **Detailed descriptions:** Provide clear and informative product descriptions that highlight features, benefits, and specifications.

- **Customer reviews:** Encourage customers to leave reviews to build trust and social proof.

### User Experience

- **Easy navigation:** Ensure your online store is easy to navigate and customers can find what they're looking for quickly.

- **Mobile-friendly design:** Optimize your store for mobile devices to provide a seamless shopping experience on all screens.

- **Fast loading times:** Ensure your website loads quickly to avoid frustrating customers and improve search engine rankings.

### Customer Service

- **Provide excellent customer support:** Respond promptly to inquiries and address any issues or concerns.

- **Offer multiple contact options:** Make it easy for customers to reach you through email, phone, or live chat.

- **Go the extra mile:** Exceed customer expectations to build loyalty and encourage repeat business.

## Marketing and Promotion

- **Track your results:** Monitor your website traffic, sales, and other key metrics to measure the effectiveness of your marketing efforts.

- **Experiment with different strategies:** Don't be afraid to try new marketing tactics and see what works best for your audience.

- **Stay up-to-date with trends:** Keep an eye on industry trends and adapt your strategies accordingly.

## Additional Tips

- **Offer secure payment options:** Build trust with customers by offering secure payment gateways.

- **Provide clear shipping and return policies:** Make sure your policies are easy to understand and accessible to customers.

- **Offer promotions and discounts:** Encourage sales with special offers and discounts.

- **Build an email list:** Use email marketing to stay connected with your customers and promote new products or offers.

By following these tips and best practices, you can create a thriving online store that provides a positive shopping experience for your customers and drives sustainable growth for your business.

## 13.9 Conclusion

Creating an online store with WordPress opens up a world of possibilities for reaching new customers and growing your business. By choosing the right e-commerce plugin, setting up your store effectively, and implementing sound marketing strategies, you can create a successful online shopping experience that drives sales and builds customer loyalty.

***

# Chapter 14: Building an LMS Website

What will you learn:



## 14.1 Introduction

The rise of online learning has opened doors for anyone with knowledge and skills to share. An **LMS (Learning Management System)** website empowers a wide range of institutions and individuals to create a powerful platform for education and training:

- **Educational Institutions:** From elementary schools to universities, LMS websites enhance traditional learning by providing online resources, interactive courses, and collaborative learning environments. Schools and colleges can extend their reach, offer flexible learning options, and personalize instruction for all students.

- **Educators:** Take your classroom expertise online and reach a wider audience beyond the physical walls of a school. Build interactive courses, deliver engaging learning materials, and connect with students on a global scale.

- **Trainers:** Offer corporate training programs, professional development courses, or specialized skill-building workshops. An LMS website streamlines course delivery, manages learner progress, and provides valuable insights into training effectiveness.

- **Entrepreneurs:** Package your expertise into online courses, workshops, or tutorials. An LMS website allows you to monetize your knowledge, build a loyal student base, and establish yourself as a leader in your field.

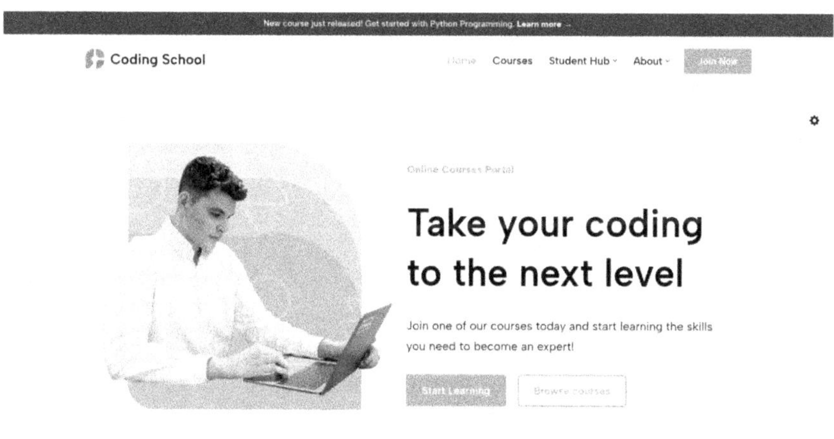


*Fig. 14.1 An LMS website demo by Neve Premium theme.*

This chapter will guide you through building an effective LMS website using WordPress and specialized plugins. We'll delve into essential features, course creation strategies, student management tools, and monetization options. With this knowledge, you can transform your expertise into a thriving online learning community.

## 14.2 Choosing an LMS Plugin

The foundation of your LMS website lies in selecting the right Learning Management System (LMS) plugin for WordPress. Several popular options exist, each with its unique features, strengths, and weaknesses. Let's explore some of the leading LMS plugins and key factors to consider when making your choice:

# 1. LearnDash

- **Strengths:** LearnDash is a comprehensive and feature-rich LMS plugin known for its robust course creation tools, advanced quizzing options, and detailed reporting features. It offers features like drip-feed content, gamification elements, and various monetization options, making it suitable for creating complex and engaging online courses.

- **Weaknesses:** LearnDash can have a steeper learning curve compared to some other LMS plugins due to its extensive features. The pricing can also be higher than other options.

- **Ideal For:** Creating complex and feature-rich online courses, professional training programs, and membership-based learning platforms.

# 2. LifterLMS

- **Strengths:** LifterLMS focuses on ease of use and flexibility, offering a user-friendly interface and drag-and-drop course builder. It integrates with various WordPress plugins and marketing tools, making it a versatile option for creating online courses and membership sites.

- **Weaknesses:** While the core plugin is free, many advanced features require purchasing add-ons, which can increase costs.

- **Ideal For:** Creating a variety of online courses, membership sites, and coaching programs with a focus on user experience and flexibility.

# 3. Tutor LMS

- **Strengths:** Tutor LMS is a user-friendly and intuitive LMS plugin with a drag-and-drop course builder, various quiz options, and built-in eCommerce features for selling courses. It offers a modern interface and a growing library of add-ons.

- **Weaknesses:** Some advanced features might require purchasing add-ons, and the plugin's community and support resources might not be as extensive as more established options.

- **Ideal For:** Creating engaging and interactive online courses with a focus on ease of use and affordability.

## 4. LearnPress

- **Strengths:** LearnPress is a free LMS plugin with basic course creation features, making it a budget-friendly option for those starting. It offers various free and premium add-ons to extend its functionalities.

- **Weaknesses:** The free version has limited features, and building a comprehensive LMS might require purchasing multiple add-ons.

- **Ideal For:** Individuals or organizations looking for a free and basic LMS solution with the option to add functionalities as needed.

Choosing the right LMS plugin sets the foundation for your online learning platform. By carefully evaluating your needs and considering the available options, you can select the plugin that best empowers you to create and deliver engaging learning experiences for your students.

# 14.3 Creating and Structuring Courses

Once you've chosen your LMS plugin, the next step is creating engaging and effective online courses. This involves selecting appropriate content formats, structuring the learning experience, and incorporating elements that keep students motivated and on track.

## Course Content Formats

- **Video Lessons:**

  - **Engaging and Visual:** Video lessons provide a dynamic and engaging way to deliver information, allowing you to demonstrate concepts, showcase examples, and connect with students on a more personal level.

  - **Creating Video Lessons:** Utilize screen recording

software, video editing tools, or even a simple smartphone camera to create video lessons.

○ **Hosting and Embedding:** Consider video hosting platforms like YouTube, Vimeo, or Wistia to host your videos and easily embed them within your courses.

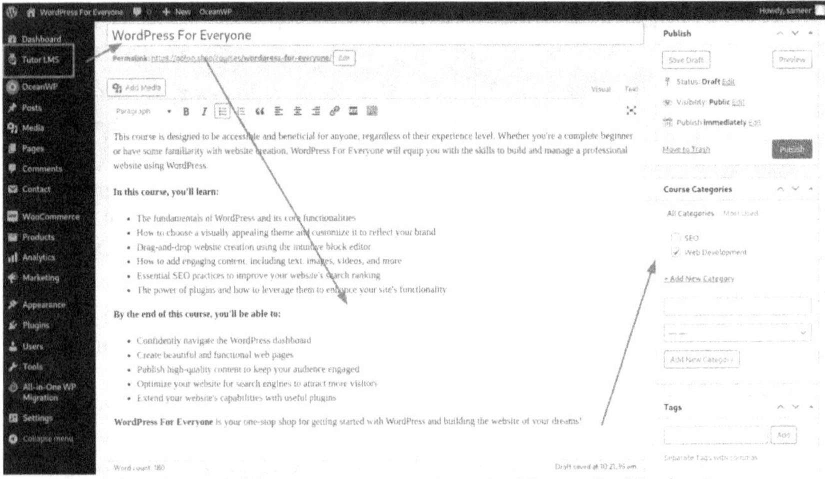

*Fig. 14.2 Adding a course using the Tutor LMS plugin.*

● **Text-Based Lessons:**

○ **Structured and Informative:** Text-based lessons provide a clear and structured format for delivering information, allowing students to learn at their own pace and easily reference key points.

○ **Engaging Text:** Make text-based lessons engaging by using headings, subheadings, bullet points, and images to break up the text and enhance readability.

○ **Multimedia Integration:** Integrate images, infographics, or audio clips to complement the text and cater to different learning styles.

● **Downloadable Resources:**

○ **Supplemental Materials:** Provide downloadable

resources like PDFs, worksheets, templates, or presentations to supplement the course content and provide students with materials they can reference offline.

- ○ **File Formats:** Offer resources in accessible formats that can be easily viewed or edited by students.

- **Quizzes and Assessments:**

  - ○ **Knowledge Checks:** Quizzes and assessments help gauge student understanding of the material and identify areas where they might need additional support.

  - ○ **Types of Assessments:** Utilize various quiz formats, such as multiple choice, true/false, fill-in-the-blank, essays, or assignments, depending on the learning objectives and content.

  - ○ **Feedback and Grading:** Provide timely feedback on quizzes and assessments to help students understand their strengths and weaknesses.

- **Interactive Elements:**

  - ○ **Engagement and Collaboration:** Incorporate interactive elements like polls, surveys, discussion forums, or live Q&A sessions to promote student engagement, collaboration, and active learning.

  - ○ **Feedback Mechanisms:** Utilize interactive elements to gather feedback from students and adapt your course content based on their needs.

## Course Structure and Organization

- **Modules and Lessons:** Break down your course content into manageable modules and lessons to provide a clear learning path and avoid overwhelming students with too much information at once.

- **Sequential or Flexible Learning:** Decide whether your course will follow a linear, sequential structure or offer a more flexible approach where students can choose the order in which they complete lessons.

- **Learning Paths:** Create different learning paths within your course to cater to students with varying skill levels or learning goals.

- **Progress Tracking:** Implement progress tracking features that allow students to visualize their advancement through the course and see their achievements. This can include progress bars, completion percentages, or checklists.

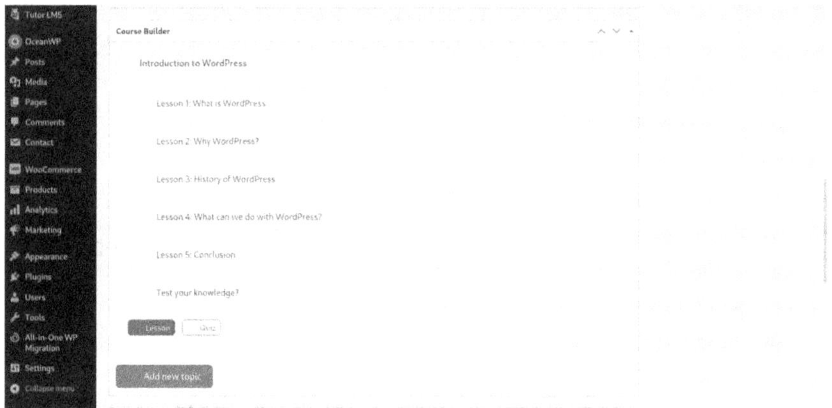


*Fig. 14.3 Adding Lessons and Quiz using the Tutor LMS plugin.*

## Additional Tips for Course Creation

- **Learning Objectives:** Clearly define learning objectives for each lesson and module to ensure students understand what they will gain from the course.

- **Variety and Engagement:** Incorporate a variety of content formats and interactive elements to keep students engaged and motivated.

- **Accessibility:** Ensure your course content is accessible to all learners, including those with disabilities.

- **Quality and Polish:** Invest time in creating high-quality course materials with professional visuals, clear audio, and error-free content.

By carefully considering the structure and format of your courses, you create a learning experience that is not only informative but also engaging, accessible, and effective in achieving your educational goals

# 14.4 Student Management and Engagement

Creating engaging courses is essential, but effectively managing your students and fostering a supportive learning environment is equally crucial for a successful LMS website. Let's explore key aspects of student management and strategies for enhancing engagement:

## Student Enrollment and Registration

- **Enrollment Options:** Determine how students will enroll in your courses. Options include:

    - **Open Enrollment:** Allow students to freely enroll in courses without restrictions.

    - **Manual Approval:** Require manual approval for student enrollments, allowing you to control access and ensure students meet prerequisites.

    - **Payment Integration:** If you're selling courses, integrate with a payment gateway to process payments during enrollment.

- **Registration Process:** Streamline the registration process to make it easy for students to sign up and access courses.

- **Student Accounts:** Provide students with individual accounts where they can manage their profiles, track progress, and access course materials.

## Communication Tools

- **Announcements:** Utilize an announcement system to share important updates, course information, or reminders with students.

- **Email Notifications:** Set up automatic email notifications to inform students about course activities, such as new lessons, upcoming deadlines, or graded assignments.

- **Discussion Forums:** Create discussion forums or online communities where students can interact with each other, ask questions, and collaborate.

- **Direct Messaging:** Enable private messaging functionalities for direct communication between instructors and students or among students.

## Progress Tracking and Reporting

- **Track Student Progress:** Monitor student progress through the course, including completion of lessons, quiz scores, and assignment submissions.

- **Reporting Tools:** Utilize reporting tools provided by your LMS plugin to generate reports on student performance, engagement, and course completion rates.

- **Individual Feedback:** Provide personalized feedback to students on their assignments, quizzes, or overall progress to support their learning journey.

- **Progress Visualization:** Consider incorporating progress bars, completion percentages, or visual representations of student achievements to motivate and provide a sense of accomplishment.

## Engagement Strategies

- **Gamification:** Implement gamification elements like badges, points, leaderboards, or rewards to incentivize participation, boost motivation, and create a sense of friendly competition among students.

- **Community Building:** Foster a sense of community among students by encouraging interactions, collaboration, and peer-to-peer support. Utilize features like discussion forums, group projects, or social media integration.

- **Personalized Learning:** Offer options for students to personalize their learning experience, such as choosing their own learning paths, setting individual goals, or selecting from different content formats.

- **Interactive Activities:** Incorporate interactive elements like quizzes, polls, simulations, or branching scenarios to keep students actively engaged in the learning process.

- **Regular Feedback:** Provide regular feedback and encouragement to students to keep them motivated and on track.

By implementing effective student management practices and incorporating engagement strategies, you create a supportive and motivating learning environment that fosters student success and enhances the overall learning experience.

## 14.5 Monetizing Your Courses (Optional)

While sharing knowledge and empowering learners is often the primary goal of creating an LMS website, you might also consider monetizing your courses to generate revenue and support the sustainability of your platform. Let's explore different approaches to monetizing your online courses:

### Selling Courses

- **eCommerce Integration:** Integrate your LMS website with an eCommerce plugin like WooCommerce to enable the sale of your courses. This allows you to set prices, process payments, and manage orders.

- **Pricing Models:** Consider different pricing models for your courses, such as:

    - **One-Time Payment**: Students pay a one-time fee for lifetime access to the course.

- ○ **Payment Plans:** Offer installment plans to make courses more affordable and accessible.

  - ○ **Subscriptions:** Implement a subscription model where students pay a recurring fee for access to multiple courses or a library of content.

- **Payment Gateways:** Integrate with secure payment gateways like Stripe, Razorpay, PayU or PayPal to process payments safely and conveniently.

- **Discounts and Promotions:** Offer discounts, promotions, or coupon codes to attract students and incentivize enrollments.

## Membership and Subscription Models

- **Membership Levels:** Create different membership tiers with varying access levels and benefits. For example, you could offer a basic membership with access to a limited number of courses and a premium membership with access to all courses and additional resources.

- **Recurring Revenue:** Membership and subscription models provide a recurring revenue stream, contributing to the long-term sustainability of your LMS platform.

- **Content Exclusivity:** Offer exclusive content or benefits to members, such as early access to new courses, bonus materials, or community features.

## Marketing and Promotions

- **Content Marketing:** Create valuable content related to your courses and share it through your website, blog, social media, and other channels to attract potential students.

- **Social Media Marketing:** Utilize social media platforms to promote your courses, engage with your audience, and run targeted ads.

- **Email Marketing:** Build an email list and utilize email marketing campaigns to nurture leads, promote new courses, and offer special discounts.

- **Affiliate Marketing:** Partner with affiliates to promote your courses and earn a commission on sales generated through their referrals.

- **Free Previews or Trials:** Offer free previews or trial periods for your courses to give students a glimpse of the content and value before they commit to purchasing.

## Monetization Strategies and Community Values***

- **Balancing Revenue and Value:** Prioritize providing value to your students and avoid excessive monetization that could compromise the learning experience.

- **Transparency and Communication:** Be transparent with your audience about your pricing, payment options, and the value they receive from your courses.

- **Ethical Considerations:** Ensure your marketing and pricing strategies are ethical and align with your values and educational goals.

Monetizing your online courses allows you to generate revenue, support the sustainability of your LMS platform, and invest in creating even better learning experiences for your students. By choosing appropriate monetization strategies and prioritizing value, you can build a successful online learning business while empowering learners and sharing your knowledge with the world.

# 14.6 Additional Features and Integrations

While your chosen LMS plugin provides the core functionalities for your online learning platform, additional features and integrations can enhance the learning experience, streamline your workflow, and offer valuable insights into student progress and engagement. Let's explore some options to consider:

## Community Features

- **Forums and Discussion Boards:** Incorporate forums or

discussion boards to facilitate interaction and collaboration among students. This allows them to ask questions, share insights, and learn from each other.

- **Social Groups:** Create social groups or communities within your LMS to foster a sense of belonging and encourage peer-to-peer support.

- **Live Chat:** Implement a live chat feature to provide real-time support and answer student questions promptly.

- **Social Media Integration:** Integrate social media platforms like Facebook or Twitter to encourage community interaction and expand your reach.

## Gamification Plugins

- **GamiPress:** A comprehensive solution for adding points, badges, ranks, and achievements to your WordPress site. It offers high customizability for rewards, challenges, and visuals.

- **myCred:** This versatile plugin focuses on a points-based system, allowing you to award points for various activities and manage them effectively. It integrates with other plugins to expand its functionality.

- **WP Optin Wheel:** Gamify your email list building with a spin-the-wheel optin form. Users can win prizes or discounts, increasing signup rates in a fun way.

- **myCred - Tutor LMS:** Specifically designed for eLearning platforms built with Tutor LMS, this plugin allows you to award points and badges for course completion and participation, fostering a more engaging learning experience.

## Video Hosting and Streaming

- **Video Hosting Platforms:** Utilize video hosting platforms like YouTube, Vimeo, or Wistia to host your video lessons and ensure smooth streaming experiences for your students.

- **Live Streaming:** Explore options for incorporating live streaming capabilities for webinars, Q&A sessions, or virtual events.

- **Interactive Video Players:** Consider using interactive video players that allow you to add quizzes, annotations, or other interactive elements to your video lessons.

## Analytics and Reporting

- **LMS Reporting Tools:** Utilize the reporting tools provided by your LMS plugin to track student progress, engagement, and course completion rates. This data provides valuable insights into the effectiveness of your courses and helps you identify areas for improvement.

- **Google Analytics Integration:** Integrate Google Analytics with your LMS website to gain deeper insights into user behavior, demographics, and traffic sources.

- **Heatmaps and User Recordings:** Consider using tools like heatmaps and user recordings to visualize how students interact with your course content and identify areas for improvement in terms of user experience and course design.

## Other Useful Integrations

- **Email Marketing Services:** Integrate your LMS with an email marketing platform like Mailchimp or ConvertKit to manage student communication, send course updates, and nurture leads.

- **CRM Integration:** Connect your LMS with a CRM system to manage student relationships, track interactions, and provide personalized support.

- **eCommerce Platforms:** Integrate with eCommerce platforms like WooCommerce or Shopify if you offer additional products or services alongside your courses.

By exploring additional features and integrations, you can enhance the functionality of your LMS website, creating a more engaging and comprehensive learning experience for your students.

## 14.7 Conclusion

Building an LMS website empowers you to become a facilitator of knowledge, sharing your expertise and making education accessible to individuals worldwide. Throughout this chapter, we explored the key steps and considerations involved in creating a successful online learning platform, from selecting the right LMS plugin and crafting engaging courses to managing student interactions and exploring monetization options.

Remember, the heart of your LMS website lies in its ability to empower learners and provide them with valuable knowledge and skills. Focus on creating high-quality courses, fostering a supportive learning environment, and utilizing technology to enhance the learning experience. As the online education landscape continues to evolve, remain adaptable, explore new trends and tools, and continuously strive to improve the value and effectiveness of your learning platform.

Building an LMS website is a rewarding endeavor that allows you to share your knowledge, empower learners, and make a positive impact on the lives of others. As you embark on this journey, remember to prioritize the needs of your students, embrace innovation, and strive to create a learning experience that is both enriching and transformative.

***

# Chapter 15: Building a Non-Profit Website

What will you learn:



## 15.1 Introduction.

Non-profit organizations play a vital role in addressing social issues, advocating for causes, and making a positive impact on communities. A well-designed website serves as a powerful tool for non-profits to raise awareness, connect with supporters, engage volunteers, and drive donations. In this chapter, we'll explore the key elements of building an effective non-profit website using WordPress, equipping you with the knowledge and strategies to amplify your organization's voice and advance your mission.

## 15.2 Choosing the Right Theme and Plugins

The foundation of your non-profit website lies in selecting the appropriate theme and plugins that align with your organization's goals and provide the necessary functionalities. Let's explore the key considerations for choosing a theme and essential plugins for your non-profit website:

### Theme Selection

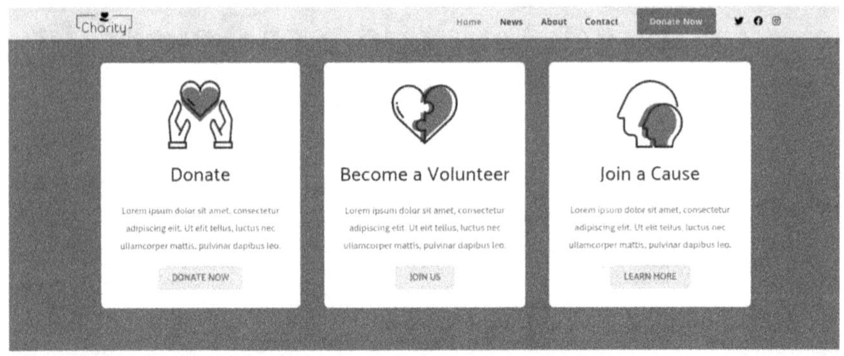


*Fig. 15.1 A Non-profit organization website demo by OceanWP Premium theme*

- **Non-Profit Themes:** Several WordPress themes are specifically designed for non-profit organizations, offering features that cater to their unique needs. These themes often include:

  - **Clean and Professional Layouts:** Non-profit themes typically feature clean, modern, and professional layouts that focus on effectively communicating the organization's mission and impact.

  - **Donation Integration:** Many non-profit themes come with built-in donation buttons or integration with popular donation plugins, making it easy for visitors to contribute financially.

  - **Event Management Features:** Some themes offer features for managing and promoting events, such as calendars, registration forms, and ticketing options.

- **Volunteer Management:** Certain themes might include features or integrations for managing volunteers and showcasing volunteer opportunities.

- **Customization Options:** Choose a theme that offers ample customization options, allowing you to tailor the design and layout to reflect your organization's branding, colors, and overall aesthetic.

- **Responsiveness and Accessibility:** Ensure the theme is responsive and mobile-friendly for optimal viewing on all devices. Additionally, prioritize themes that prioritize accessibility features to cater to users with disabilities.

## Essential Plugins for Non-Profit Websites

- **Donation Plugins:**

  - **GiveWP:** A popular and user-friendly donation plugin that allows you to create customizable donation forms, manage donors, track donations, and generate reports.

  - **Charitable:** Another popular option with features like recurring donations, peer-to-peer fundraising, and donor management tools.

  - **Donorbox:** A feature-rich donation platform with options for recurring donations, donor profiles, company gift matching, and various integrations.

- **Event Management Plugins :**

  - **The Events Calendar:** A comprehensive event management plugin that allows you to create and manage events, display calendars, sell tickets, and track registrations.

  - **Event Espresso:** Another popular option with features like event ticketing, registration management, and email marketing integrations.

- **Volunteer Management Plugins:**

  - **WPForms or Gravity Forms:** These popular form builder plugins can be used to create volunteer registration forms, collect volunteer information, and manage volunteer applications.

○ **Wired Impact Volunteer Management:** A dedicated plugin specifically designed for managing volunteers, offering features like volunteer profiles, scheduling, and communication tools.

- **Additional Plugins to Consider:**

  ○ **Social Media Sharing Plugins:** Make it easy for visitors to share your content and engage with your organization on social media.

  ○ **Email Marketing Plugins:** Integrate your website with an email marketing platform to manage your subscriber list, send newsletters, and communicate with supporters.

  ○ **Analytics Plugins:** Gain insights into your website traffic and user behavior with analytics plugins like MonsterInsights.

Choosing the right theme and plugins for your non-profit website is crucial for creating a user-friendly platform that effectively communicates your mission, engages your supporters, and facilitates donations and volunteer participation. By carefully considering your organization's specific needs and goals, you can select the tools that empower you to make a meaningful impact online.

# 15.3 Essential Pages for a Non-Profit Website

The content and structure of your non-profit website play a crucial role in effectively communicating your mission, engaging your audience, and inspiring action. Let's explore the essential pages that every non-profit website should include:

## 1. Homepage

- **Mission and Impact:** The homepage should prominently display your organization's mission statement and clearly communicate the impact you make on the community or cause you serve.

- **Compelling Visuals:** Utilize high-quality images or videos that showcase your work, evoke emotions, and resonate with your target audience.

- **Call to Action:** Include prominent and clear calls to action that guide visitors towards desired actions, such as donating, volunteering, or signing up for your newsletter.

- **Navigation:** Ensure your homepage has clear and intuitive navigation that allows visitors to easily access other essential pages on your website.

## 2. About Us

- **Story and History:** Share your organization's story, highlighting its origins, founders, and the journey that led to its current mission.

- **Team and Staff:** Introduce your team members, staff, and board of directors, showcasing their expertise and dedication to the cause.

- **Transparency and Financials:** Provide information about your organization's financial health, including annual reports, impact reports, and information about how donations are used. This transparency builds trust and credibility with potential donors and supporters.

- **Values and Beliefs:** Clearly articulate your organization's core values and beliefs to connect with individuals who share your vision.

## 3. Programs and Services

- **Showcase Your Impact:** Highlight the programs and services your organization offers, emphasizing their impact on the community and the individuals you serve. Use compelling descriptions, images, and videos to showcase the positive outcomes of your work.

- **Success Stories and Testimonials:** Share success stories and testimonials from individuals or communities who have benefited from your organization's work. This provides social proof and demonstrates the real-world impact of your efforts.

- **Program-Specific Pages:** Create dedicated pages for each of your programs or services, providing detailed information about their goals, activities, and outcomes.

## 4. Get Involved

- **Volunteer Opportunities:** Clearly outline volunteer opportunities available within your organization, including descriptions of roles, time commitments, and the impact volunteers can make. Provide an easy-to-use volunteer registration form to streamline the process.

- **Donation Options:** Make it simple for individuals to donate by providing various donation options, including one-time donations, recurring donations, and information about other ways to contribute, such as planned giving or in-kind donations.

- **Events Calendar:** Promote upcoming events and provide a calendar with detailed information about each event, including dates, times, locations, and registration options.

## 5. Additional Pages to Consider

- **News and Blog:** Share news, updates, and stories about your organization's work to keep your audience informed and engaged.

- **Resources and FAQs:** Provide resources or frequently asked questions related to your cause or the services you offer.

- **Contact Us:** Make it easy for visitors to contact your organization with any questions or inquiries.

By including these essential pages on your non-profit website, you effectively communicate your mission, showcase your impact, and provide clear pathways for individuals to get involved and support your cause. Remember to maintain a user-friendly and accessible website, update content regularly, and optimize for search engines to ensure your website reaches a wider audience and maximizes its impact.

# 15.4 Engaging Your Supporters and Volunteers

Building a strong and engaged community of supporters and volunteers is essential for the long-term success of any non-profit organization. Your website plays a crucial role in fostering these relationships and creating opportunities for meaningful engagement.

## Storytelling and Impact Communication

- **Share Compelling Stories:** Connect with your audience on an emotional level by sharing compelling stories about the individuals or communities impacted by your organization's work. Use vivid descriptions, powerful images, and videos to showcase the positive changes you're making.

- **Highlight Individual Journeys:** Feature stories of individuals who have benefited from your programs or services, showcasing their challenges, successes, and the transformative impact of your organization's support.

- **Data and Impact Reports:** While storytelling is powerful, also provide data and impact reports to demonstrate the effectiveness of your programs and the tangible outcomes you achieve.

- **Transparency and Authenticity:** Be transparent about your challenges and successes, and communicate with authenticity to build trust and credibility with your audience.

## Volunteer Management

- **Recruitment and Onboarding:** Streamline the volunteer recruitment process by providing clear information about volunteer opportunities, creating an easy-to-use application form, and implementing an efficient onboarding process to welcome new volunteers.

- **Volunteer Profiles and Matching:** Consider incorporating a volunteer management system or plugin that allows volunteers to create profiles, highlight their skills and interests, and match them with suitable volunteer opportunities.

- **Scheduling and Communication:** Utilize tools for scheduling volunteer shifts, sending reminders, and facilitating communication between staff and volunteers.

- **Recognition and Appreciation:** Express gratitude and appreciation for your volunteers' contributions through regular communication, recognition events, or volunteer spotlights on your website or social media.

## Donor Recognition and Appreciation

- **Personalized Thank You Messages:** Send personalized thank you messages to donors immediately after they contribute, expressing your gratitude and acknowledging their support.

- **Impact Updates:** Keep donors informed about how their contributions are making a difference by sharing impact updates, success stories, and program reports.

- **Donor Recognition Programs:** Consider implementing donor recognition programs, such as acknowledging major donors on your website or in annual reports, to show appreciation and incentivize continued support.

- **Exclusive Events or Content:** Offer exclusive events, webinars, or content for donors as a token of appreciation and a way to deepen their engagement with your organization.

## News and Updates

- **Regular Communication:** Keep your supporters and volunteers informed about your activities, upcoming events, and recent accomplishments through regular communication channels, such as:

  - O **Blog Posts:** Share updates, stories, and insights related to your organization's work.

  - O **Newsletters:** Send regular email newsletters with news, events, and calls to action.

- ○ **Social Media Updates:** Utilize social media platforms to share timely updates, engage with your audience, and promote your initiatives.

- **Impact Reports:** Publish annual or periodic impact reports that highlight your achievements, progress towards goals, and the positive outcomes of your work.

- **Transparency and Accountability:** Demonstrate transparency by sharing financial information, governance policies, and impact data with your supporters.

Engaging your supporters and volunteers requires ongoing effort and a genuine commitment to building relationships. By implementing these strategies, you can foster a strong community around your cause, inspire action, and empower individuals to contribute to your mission in meaningful ways.

# 15.5 Fundraising Strategies and Tools

Fundraising is a critical aspect of most non-profit organizations, providing the resources needed to sustain operations and fulfill their missions. Your website plays a crucial role in facilitating donations and implementing effective fundraising strategies. Let's explore various approaches and tools to enhance your fundraising efforts:

## Online Donation Platforms

- **Donation Plugins:** Utilize dedicated donation plugins like GiveWP, Charitable, or Donorbox to create customizable donation forms, process online payments securely, and manage donor information.

- **Recurring Donations:** Encourage recurring donations by offering options for donors to contribute automatically on a regular basis (e.g., monthly or annually). This provides a predictable and sustainable source of funding for your organization.

- **Donation Tiers and Impact:** Consider offering different donation tiers with varying levels of impact or recognition to incentivize larger contributions.

- **Matching Gifts:** Promote matching gift programs where companies match their employees' donations, effectively doubling the impact of individual contributions.

- **Tribute Donations:** Allow donors to make donations in honor or memory of someone special, providing a meaningful way to contribute and honor loved ones.

## Crowdfunding Campaigns

- **Project-Based Fundraising:** Utilize crowdfunding platforms like Kickstarter or GoFundMe to raise funds for specific projects or initiatives.

- **Peer-to-Peer Fundraising:** Empower your supporters to create their own fundraising campaigns on your behalf, expanding your reach and engaging a wider network of potential donors.

- **Compelling Campaigns:** Craft compelling crowdfunding campaigns with clear goals, engaging storytelling, and impactful visuals to attract potential donors.

## Matching Gifts and Corporate Sponsorships

- **Matching Gift Programs:** Research and promote matching gift programs offered by companies to encourage employees to double their donations.

- **Corporate Sponsorships:** Seek partnerships with corporations that align with your mission and values, securing sponsorships for events, programs, or general operations.

- **Cause Marketing:** Explore cause marketing partnerships with businesses, where a portion of sales from specific products or services are donated to your organization.

## Additional Fundraising Tools and Strategies

- **Events:** Organize fundraising events such as galas, auctions, or benefit concerts to engage your community and raise funds.

- **Merchandise:** Create and sell branded merchandise, such as t-shirts, mugs, or tote bags, to generate revenue and promote your organization.

- **Grants:** Research and apply for grants from foundations or government agencies that support your cause or programs.

- **Planned Giving:** Offer information about planned giving options, such as bequests or charitable trusts, to encourage long-term support.

## Promoting Your Fundraising Efforts

- **Website Integration:** Integrate donation buttons and information about your fundraising initiatives throughout your website, including your homepage, program pages, and blog posts.

- **Email Marketing:** Utilize email marketing to share fundraising appeals, impact stories, and updates on your progress towards goals.

- **Social Media:** Promote your fundraising campaigns on social media platforms and encourage sharing to reach a wider audience.

- **Community Outreach:** Engage with your local community through events, presentations, and partnerships to raise awareness and attract potential donors.

Effective fundraising requires a multi-faceted approach that combines online tools, strategic planning, and community engagement. By implementing these strategies and utilizing the available tools, you can secure the resources needed to sustain your non-profit organization and continue making a positive impact on the world.

# 15.6 Conclusion

A non-profit website serves as a vital tool for amplifying your organization's voice, connecting with supporters, and advancing your mission. By implementing the strategies and considerations discussed in this chapter, you can create a website that effectively communicates your story, inspires action, and empowers you to make a lasting difference in the world.

Remember, your website is not just an online brochure; it's a dynamic platform for engagement, fundraising, and community building. Continuously evaluate your website's performance, gather feedback from your audience, and adapt your strategies to ensure your online presence remains impactful and relevant.

Building a non-profit website requires a commitment to your mission, a deep understanding of your audience, and a willingness to adapt and evolve as your organization grows. By embracing the power of digital tools and implementing effective strategies, you can create a website that becomes a catalyst for positive change and empowers you to achieve your goals.

***

# Chapter 16: Creating a Resume/Portfolio Website

What will you learn:



## 16.1 Introduction

In today's competitive job market and dynamic freelance landscape, a strong online presence is no longer optional – it's essential. Your resume/portfolio website serves as your digital first impression, showcasing your skills, experience, and personality to potential employers, clients, or collaborators across the globe. It's a space where you can go beyond the limitations of a traditional resume and truly express your unique value proposition.

### Why a Resume/Portfolio Website Matters

- **Control Your Narrative:** Unlike a static resume, your website allows you to control the narrative and present your skills and experiences in a way that aligns with your personal brand and career goals.

- **Showcase Your Work:** Go beyond simply listing your work experience and showcase your projects, accomplishments, and creative talents through engaging visuals and detailed descriptions.

- **Demonstrate Your Expertise:** Position yourself as an expert in your field by sharing your knowledge, insights, and thought leadership through blog posts, articles, or case studies.

- **Accessibility and Reach:** Make your information easily accessible to potential employers or clients anywhere in the world, 24/7.

- **Personal Branding:** Craft a unique online presence that reflects your personality, values, and professional aspirations.

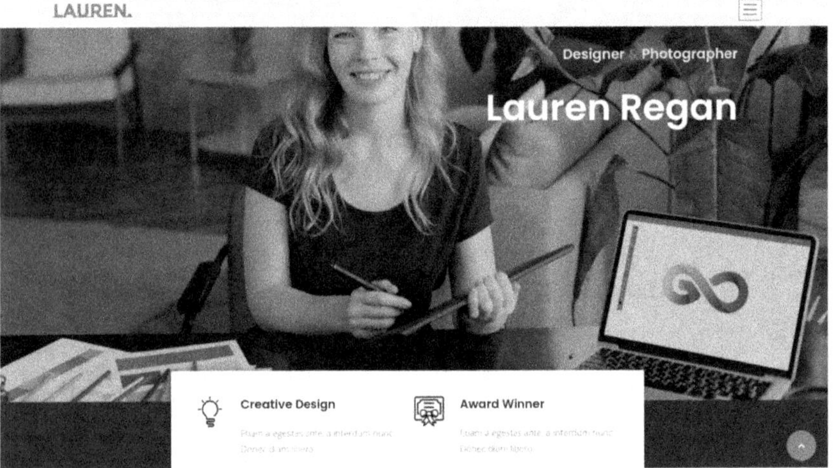


*Fig. 16.1 a resume website demo by OceanWP Premium theme.*

## For Who

- **Creative Professionals:** Designers, photographers, writers, artists, musicians, and other creatives can showcase their portfolios and attract potential clients.

- **Freelancers and Consultants:** Independent professionals can use their websites to highlight their services, expertise, and client testimonials.

- **Job Seekers:** Individuals seeking new employment opportunities can create a more comprehensive and engaging presentation of their qualifications beyond a traditional resume.

- **Entrepreneurs and Business Owners:** Showcase your business, products, services, and team members to potential investors, partners, or customers.

- **Students and Recent Graduates:** Build an online presence early in your career and showcase your academic achievements, skills, and projects to potential employers.

- **Anyone Seeking to Build a Personal Brand:** Establish your expertise, thought leadership, and online presence within your industry or niche.

Regardless of your profession or career stage, a resume/portfolio website can be a valuable tool for advancing your goals and creating opportunities. In this chapter, we'll explore the steps to build a compelling and effective website that showcases your unique talents and sets you apart from the competition.

# 16.2 Choosing the Right Theme and Plugins

The foundation of your resume/portfolio website lies in selecting the appropriate theme and plugins that align with your goals and provide the necessary functionalities. Let's explore key considerations for choosing a theme and essential plugins for your website:

## Theme Selection

- **Portfolio Themes:** Many WordPress themes are specifically designed for portfolio websites, offering features like:

    - **Visually Appealing Layouts:** Portfolio themes prioritize visual presentation with grid layouts, galleries, and full-screen image displays to showcase your work effectively.

    - **Project Showcase Options:** Look for themes that offer various project showcase options, such as sliders, carousels, or masonry grids, to present your work in an engaging and organized manner.

- **Customization Options:** Choose a theme that allows you to personalize the design, layout, and colors to reflect your personal brand and style.

- **Resume Themes:** Some themes are tailored for online resumes, emphasizing clean and professional design with features like:

  - **Clear and Organized Layout:** Resume themes prioritize clear presentation of your experience, skills, and education with well-structured sections and easy-to-read typography.

  - **Timeline Features:** Look for themes that offer timeline features to showcase your career progression and accomplishments in a visually appealing manner.

  - **Downloadable Resume Option:** Choose a theme that allows you to offer a downloadable version of your resume in PDF format.

- **Multi-Purpose Themes:** Consider versatile multi-purpose themes that offer flexibility for creating both portfolio and resume sections within the same website. This provides a comprehensive presentation of your skills and experience.

## Essential Plugins for Resume/Portfolio Websites

- **Portfolio Plugins:**

  - **Envira Gallery:** A popular plugin for creating responsive image and video galleries with various layouts, lightbox options, and customization features.

  - **Portfolio Gallery:** Another versatile plugin with options for creating grid-based or masonry portfolio layouts, filtering projects by category, and adding lightbox effects.

- **Page Builder Plugins:**

  - **Elementor:** A powerful drag-and-drop page builder that allows you to create custom layouts, add various elements, and design unique pages without coding knowledge.

- ○ **Beaver Builder:** Another popular page builder with a user-friendly interface and a wide range of modules and templates for creating custom layouts.

● **Contact Form Plugins:**

- ○ **Contact Form 7:** A widely used and free plugin offering basic contact form functionalities with customizable fields and email notifications.

- ○ **WPForms:** A user-friendly plugin with a drag-and-drop form builder, pre-built templates, and advanced features like conditional logic and file uploads.

● **Additional Plugins to Consider:**

- ○ **SEO Plugins:** Optimize your website for search engines with plugins like Yoast SEO or Rank Math.

- ○ **Social Media Sharing Plugins:** Make it easy for visitors to share your work and connect with you on social media.

- ○ **Analytics Plugins:** Gain insights into your website traffic and user behavior with analytics plugins like MonsterInsights.

Choosing the right theme and plugins is crucial for building a visually appealing, functional, and engaging resume/portfolio website. By carefully considering your needs and exploring the available options, you can create a platform that effectively showcases your talents and attracts opportunities.

# 16.3 Essential Pages for Your Website

The content and structure of your resume/portfolio website play a crucial role in effectively presenting your skills, experience, and personality to potential employers or clients. Let's explore the essential pages that every resume/portfolio website should include:

## Showcase

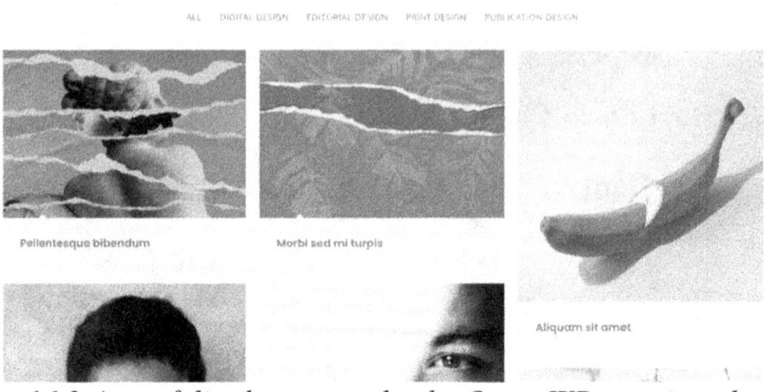


*Fig. 16.2 A portfolio demo page by the OceanWP premium theme.*

# 1. Homepage

- **Introduction and Branding:** Create a strong first impression with a clear and engaging headline that introduces you and your area of expertise. Include a concise bio that highlights your key skills and experiences.

- **Visual Appeal:** Utilize a visually appealing design with high-quality images or videos that showcase your work, personality, or brand identity.

- **Call to Action:** Guide visitors towards desired actions with a prominent call to action, such as "View My Portfolio," "Contact Me," or "Learn More About My Services."

- **Navigation:** Ensure your homepage has clear and intuitive navigation that allows visitors to easily access other essential pages on your website.

## 2. Portfolio

- **Project Showcases:** Dedicate a section or create individual pages to showcase your best work. Include high-quality images, videos, or other media that effectively represent each project.

- **Project Descriptions:** Provide detailed descriptions of your projects, highlighting your role, the skills utilized, the challenges faced, and the project's outcomes or impact.

- **Categorization and Filtering:** Organize your portfolio by category, skills, or project type to facilitate easy navigation and allow visitors to quickly find relevant work examples.

- **Visual Appeal:** Prioritize a visually appealing and engaging layout for your portfolio, using grids, sliders, or other design elements to showcase your work effectively.

## 3. Resume/CV

- **Work Experience:** Present your work experience in reverse chronological order, including company names, job titles, dates of employment, and descriptions of your responsibilities and achievements. Quantify your accomplishments with data or metrics whenever possible.

- **Skills and Expertise:** Highlight your key skills and areas of expertise, using visual representations like progress bars or skill charts to showcase your proficiency levels.

- **Education and Certifications:** Include information about your educational background, degrees earned, relevant coursework, and any certifications or professional development you've completed.

- **Awards and Recognition:** Showcase any awards, accolades, or recognition you've received to demonstrate your achievements and expertise.

- **Downloadable Resume Option:** Offer a downloadable version of your resume in PDF format for potential employers or clients to easily save or print.

## 4. About Me

- **Personal Branding:** Share your personal story, values, and motivations to connect with your audience on a deeper level and build a personal brand that resonates with potential employers or clients.

- **Interests and Hobbies:** Consider including information about your interests or hobbies to showcase your personality and well-roundedness.

- **Professional Photo:** Include a professional headshot to present a polished and approachable image.

## 5. Contact

- **Contact Information:** Provide clear and accessible contact information, including your email address, phone number, and links to your social media profiles.

- **Contact Form:** Include a contact form to make it easy for potential employers or clients to reach out to you directly.

## 6. Additional Pages to Consider

- **Blog:** Share your insights, expertise, and thought leadership through a blog to establish yourself as an authority in your field and attract a wider audience.

- **Testimonials:** If available, include testimonials from past clients, colleagues, or employers to build credibility and showcase positive feedback.

- **Services:** If you're a freelancer or consultant, dedicate a page to outlining the services you offer and your rates or pricing structure.

By strategically structuring your resume/portfolio website and including these essential pages, you create a comprehensive and engaging platform that effectively showcases your skills, experience, and personality to potential employers or clients.

# 16.4 Showcasing Your Work Effectively

A strong portfolio is the heart of your resume/portfolio website, serving as a visual representation of your skills, experience, and creative abilities. Effectively showcasing your work is crucial for capturing attention, making a lasting impression, and convincing potential employers or clients of your capabilities.

## High-Quality Visuals

- **Professional Images and Videos:** Utilize high-resolution images, videos, or other media that showcase your work in the best possible light. Invest in professional photography or videography if necessary, especially if your field relies heavily on visual presentation.

- **Variety of Media:** Incorporate a variety of media formats to keep your portfolio engaging and cater to different learning styles. This could include images, videos, audio clips, interactive elements, or even 3D models.

- **Visual Storytelling:** Use visuals to tell a story about each project, showcasing the process, challenges, and outcomes in a compelling way.

## Project Descriptions

- **Clear and Concise:** Provide clear and concise descriptions of your projects, highlighting the key objectives, your role, the skills utilized, and the project's impact or results.

- **Quantifiable Achievements:** Whenever possible, quantify your achievements with data or metrics to demonstrate the tangible outcomes of your work.

- **Keywords and Skills:** Incorporate relevant keywords and skills throughout your project descriptions to improve search engine optimization (SEO) and make it easier for potential employers or clients to find your work.

## Case Studies

- **In-Depth Analysis:** For selected projects, consider creating in-depth case studies that provide a comprehensive overview of the project, including the client's needs, the challenges faced, the solutions implemented, and the final results.

- **Process and Methodology:** Showcase your problem-solving skills and work process by outlining the steps taken to complete the project, from initial concept to final delivery.

- **Visuals and Data:** Utilize visuals like charts, graphs, and images to support your case study and demonstrate the impact of your work.

## Testimonials

- **Social Proof:** Include testimonials from satisfied clients, colleagues, or employers to provide social proof and build credibility.

- **Variety of Sources:** Gather testimonials from diverse sources to showcase your range of skills and experience.

- **Visual Representation:** Consider incorporating headshots or logos alongside testimonials to add a personal touch and enhance credibility.

## Additional Tips for Showcasing Your Work

- **Curate Your Portfolio:** Select only your best and most relevant work to include in your portfolio. Quality over quantity is key.

- **Target Your Audience:** Tailor your portfolio to your target audience and the types of projects or clients you want to attract.

- **Keep it Updated:** Regularly update your portfolio with your latest and most impressive work to demonstrate your ongoing growth and development.

- **Accessibility:** Ensure your portfolio is accessible to all users, including those with disabilities, by providing alternative text for images and using clear and concise language.

By effectively showcasing your work through high-quality visuals, compelling descriptions, and insightful case studies, you can capture the attention of potential employers or clients and demonstrate the value you bring to the table. Remember, your portfolio is a dynamic representation of your skills and abilities, so keep it updated, relevant, and reflective of your evolving expertise.

# 16.5 Optimizing for Visibility and Opportunities

Building a well-designed resume/portfolio website is essential, but it's equally important to ensure that potential employers or clients can easily find you online. Optimizing your website for visibility and actively seeking out opportunities are crucial steps in advancing your career goals.

## Search Engine Optimization (SEO)

- **Keyword Research:** Identify relevant keywords that potential employers or clients might use to search for someone with your skills and experience. Use keyword research tools like Google Keyword Planner or SEMrush to discover search volume and competition levels.

- **Optimize Page Titles and Meta Descriptions:** Craft clear and concise page titles and meta descriptions that accurately reflect your website content and incorporate relevant keywords. This helps search engines understand your website and improves its ranking in search results.

- **Optimize Content:** Incorporate relevant keywords throughout your website content, including page headings, project descriptions, and blog posts. However, prioritize natural language and readability over keyword stuffing.

- **Image Optimization:** Optimize your images by using descriptive file names and alt text that include relevant keywords. This helps search engines understand your images and improves their visibility in image search results.

## Social Media Integration

- **Promote Your Website:** Share your website and individual projects on your social media profiles to reach a wider audience and connect with potential employers or clients.

- **Engage with Your Audience:** Actively engage with your followers, participate in relevant industry discussions, and share valuable content related to your field.

- **Build a Following:** Grow your social media following by consistently posting engaging content, interacting with other users, and utilizing relevant hashtags.

## Networking and Outreach

- **Connect with Professionals:** Utilize online platforms like LinkedIn to connect with professionals in your industry, join relevant groups, and participate in discussions.

- **Reach Out to Potential Clients or Employers:** Identify potential clients or employers and proactively reach out to them, showcasing your work and expressing your interest in opportunities.

- **Attend Industry Events:** Attend industry conferences, workshops, or networking events to connect with people in person and build relationships.

## Online Portfolio Platforms

- **Expand Your Reach:** Create profiles on online portfolio platforms like Behance, Dribbble, or Coroflot to showcase your work to a wider audience and connect with other creative professionals.

- **Targeted Exposure:** These platforms often cater to specific creative fields, allowing you to target your portfolio towards relevant audiences and potential clients.

- **Community Engagement:** Participate in online communities within these platforms to network, collaborate, and learn from other professionals.

## Additional Tips for Visibility

- **Guest Blogging:** Contribute guest posts to other blogs or online publications within your industry to expand your reach and establish yourself as an expert.

- **Online Directories:** List your website or portfolio in online directories relevant to your field.

- **Collaborations:** Collaborate with other professionals on projects or initiatives to expand your network and gain exposure to new audiences.

Optimizing your website for visibility and actively seeking out opportunities are crucial for maximizing the impact of your online presence and achieving your career goals. By combining SEO strategies, social media engagement, networking, and participation in online communities, you can effectively showcase your talents and attract exciting opportunities in your field.

# 16.6 Conclusion

Your resume/portfolio website is more than just a collection of your work; it's a powerful tool for building your online brand and shaping the way you present yourself to the world. By implementing the strategies and considerations discussed in this chapter, you can create a website that effectively showcases your skills, attracts opportunities, and propels you towards your career aspirations.

Remember, your online presence is an ongoing journey, not a destination. Continuously update your website with your latest projects, refine your personal brand, and engage with your audience to build meaningful connections and establish yourself as a leader in your field.

***

# Part 4

# Resources and Next Steps

# Chapter 17: Troubleshooting and FAQs

What will you learn:



## 17.1 Introduction

Congratulations! You've embarked on an exciting journey into the world of WordPress, building and customizing your website with creativity and confidence. As you explore the vast possibilities of this platform, it's important to remember that challenges and occasional hiccups are a natural part of the process.

While WordPress empowers users of all skill levels, encountering technical issues or unexpected behavior can be frustrating. The good news is that most problems have solutions, and developing your troubleshooting skills will equip you to overcome these hurdles and keep your website running smoothly.

This chapter will be your guide to navigating common WordPress challenges. We'll delve into identifying problems, understanding error messages, and implementing effective solutions. From theme conflicts to plugin glitches, security concerns, and performance hiccups, we'll explore practical strategies to diagnose and resolve various issues.

**Remember**, even the most experienced WordPress users encounter occasional roadblocks. Embrace these challenges as opportunities to learn and grow your skills. By equipping yourself with the knowledge and tools in this chapter, you'll be well-prepared to tackle any obstacle and confidently manage your WordPress website.

# 17.2 Identifying and Diagnosing Problems

When your WordPress website throws a curveball, knowing how to identify and diagnose the problem is the first step towards a solution. Just like a detective gathering clues, you'll need to investigate the symptoms, analyze the evidence, and narrow down the potential culprits. Let's explore some key strategies for effective WordPress troubleshooting:

## 1. Deciphering Error Messages

WordPress often provides valuable clues in the form of error messages. Pay close attention to the wording and any error codes displayed. These messages can point you towards the source of the issue, whether it's a plugin conflict, a theme issue, or a server-side problem.

## 2. Isolating Conflicts

Theme and plugin conflicts are common culprits behind WordPress issues. To isolate the source, try deactivating all plugins and switching to a default theme like Twenty Twenty-Three. If the problem disappears, reactivate plugins one by one or switch themes systematically to identify the conflicting element.

## 3. Utilizing Browser Developer Tools

Modern web browsers offer powerful developer tools that allow you to inspect website elements, analyze network requests, and identify front-end issues. Learn to use the "Inspect Element" feature to examine HTML and CSS code and troubleshoot layout or styling problems.

## 4. WordPress Debug Mode

For more advanced troubleshooting, enabling WordPress's debug mode can be invaluable. This mode displays PHP errors and warnings that might be hidden by default. However, use caution as debug mode can reveal sensitive information; it's best to enable it only when actively troubleshooting and disable it afterward.

## 5. Check for Recent Changes

Often, problems arise after making changes to your website. Consider any recent updates to WordPress core, themes, plugins, or even custom code. Reverting these changes can sometimes quickly resolve the issue.

## 6. Review Error Logs

Your web hosting provider might offer access to server error logs, which can provide detailed information about PHP errors, database issues, or other server-side problems.

## 7. Seek Community Support

The WordPress community is a vast and helpful resource. Online forums, support groups, and documentation can offer valuable insights and solutions to common problems. Don't hesitate to seek help from experienced users or developers if you're stuck.

By mastering these detective skills, you'll be well-equipped to identify the root cause of WordPress issues and implement the appropriate solutions, ensuring your website runs smoothly and efficiently.

# 17.3 Common WordPress Errors & Solutions

Now that you're equipped with detective skills, let's tackle some of the most common WordPress errors you might encounter. Remember, these are just starting points, and further investigation might be needed depending on your specific situation.

## Internal Server Error

This generic error message often indicates a problem with the website's server.

**Solutions**:

1. **Deactivate all plugins:** This helps identify if a plugin is causing the error. Reactivate them one by one to pinpoint the culprit. To manually deactivate the plugin you need to browse file manager, and locate subfolder 'plugin' in 'wp-content' folder and rename it, temporarily.

2. **Switch to a default theme:** Rule out theme-related issues by temporarily switching to a default WordPress theme like Twenty

Twenty-Three.

3. **Increase PHP memory limit:** Sometimes, the error occurs due to insufficient memory allocated to PHP. Contact your hosting provider for assistance with increasing the limit.

4. **Check file permissions:** Incorrect file permissions can cause server errors. Ensure your WordPress files and folders have the appropriate permissions.

5. **Review server error logs:** These logs, often provided by your hosting provider, can offer more specific clues about the server-side issue.

## Error Establishing a Database Connection

This error means WordPress cannot communicate with your website's database.

**Solutions:**

1. **Verify database credentials:** Ensure the database name, username, and password in your wp-config.php file are correct.

2. **Check database server:** Contact your hosting provider to verify if the database server is functioning properly.

3. **Repair the database:** WordPress includes a database repair feature. Try accessing it by adding define('WP_ALLOW_REPAIR', true); to your wp-config.php file and visiting the repair page.

## White Screen of Death

This dreaded error displays a blank white screen with no information, often caused by PHP errors or exhausted memory limits.

**Solutions:**

1. **Deactivate all plugins:** Similar to the Internal Server Error, start by deactivating all plugins to isolate the issue.

2. **Switch to a default theme:** Rule out theme-related problems by

temporarily switching themes.

3. **Enable debug mode:** This will display PHP errors on the white screen, providing clues about the cause.

4. **Increase PHP memory limit:** If the error is due to insufficient memory, increasing the PHP memory limit might resolve it.

## 404 Not Found Error

This error indicates that the requested page cannot be found.

**Solutions:**

- **Check permalink settings:** Ensure your permalink structure is set up correctly (generally 'post name') and resave the settings.

- **Fix broken links:** Identify and correct any broken links within your website content or menus.

- **Redirect missing pages:** If a page has been deleted or moved, set up redirects to guide visitors to the correct location.

## Maintenance Mode Error

After a WordPress update, your website might get stuck in maintenance mode.

**Solutions:** Manually remove .maintenance file: Access your website files via FTP or your hosting file manager and delete the .maintenance file.

**Remember,** troubleshooting is often a process of elimination. By systematically trying these solutions and using the diagnostic tools mentioned earlier, you'll be able to effectively identify and resolve common WordPress errors and keep your website functioning smoothly.

## 17.4 Security Troubleshooting

Website security is paramount, and WordPress, being a popular platform, can sometimes be targeted by malicious actors. While preventative measures are crucial, knowing how to identify and respond to security issues is equally important.

# Recognizing the Signs of a Hacked Website

- **Unexpected Redirects:** Visitors are redirected to spam or malicious websites.

- **Defaced Website:** The appearance of your website is altered, often with unwanted messages or images.

- **Spam Content:** Spam comments, posts, or users appear on your website.

- **Unfamiliar Files or Code:** You discover unknown files or code within your WordPress installation.

- **Performance Issues:** A sudden drop in website performance or unusual server activity might indicate malware.

- **Blacklisting:** Your website is flagged as unsafe by search engines or security software.

# Immediate Actions After a Hack

1. **Change Passwords:** Immediately change all WordPress passwords, including administrator accounts, FTP access, and database credentials.

2. **Scan for Malware:** Utilize security plugins or online scanning tools to detect and remove malicious code from your website.

3. **Restore from Backup:** If you have recent backups, consider restoring your website to a clean state before the hack.

4. **Update WordPress & Plugins:** Ensure you're using the latest versions of WordPress core, themes, and plugins to patch any vulnerabilities.

5. **Seek Professional Help:** If you're unable to resolve the hack on your own, consider seeking assistance from a security expert or your hosting provider.

# Security Hardening Tips

- **Strong Passwords:** Enforce strong password policies for all user accounts and avoid using easily guessable passwords.

- **Regular Updates:** Keep WordPress core, themes, and plugins updated to benefit from the latest security patches.

- **Limit Login Attempts:** Use plugins to limit login attempts and prevent brute force attacks.

- **Two-Factor Authentication:** Implement two-factor authentication for an extra layer of security during login.

- **Security Plugins:** Utilize reputable security plugins to scan for vulnerabilities, monitor activity, and implement additional security measures.

- **Regular Backups:** Create regular backups of your website to ensure you can restore it in case of a security incident.

By remaining vigilant, taking swift action when necessary, and implementing preventive measures, you can safeguard your WordPress website and protect your valuable online presence.

# 17.5 FAQs

While we've covered many fundamental aspects of WordPress throughout this book, there are always more questions to explore. Let's delve into some frequently asked questions that delve beyond the basics and address specific scenarios you might encounter:

## 1. What is a staging website, and why is it important?

**A:** A staging website is a separate copy of your live website where you can safely test changes, updates, or new features without affecting your live site. It's an invaluable tool for experimenting with designs, plugins, or code modifications before implementing them on your public website, minimizing the risk of errors or disruptions.

## 2. Can I create an Android app from my WordPress website?

**A:** Absolutely! Several methods exist for converting your WordPress website into a mobile app. Some plugins specialize in app creation, offering features like content syncing, push notifications, and offline access. Alternatively, you can explore app development platforms that integrate with WordPress or consider hiring a developer for a custom solution.

## 3. What coding languages should I learn to become a WordPress expert?

**A:** While you can achieve a lot with WordPress without coding, learning some basic languages can significantly expand your capabilities. Start with HTML and CSS to understand website structure and styling. Then, delve into PHP, the language behind WordPress, to create custom themes, plugins, and functionality. JavaScript knowledge can further enhance interactivity and user experience.

## 4. How can I create my own WordPress plugin or theme?

**A:** Creating plugins and themes requires coding knowledge and an understanding of WordPress development principles. Start by learning PHP, HTML, CSS, and JavaScript. The WordPress Codex offers extensive documentation and resources for developers. Numerous online tutorials and courses can guide you through the process of building your own plugins and themes.

## 5. My theme or plugin is not publishing new updates. What should I do?

**A:** If you've made changes to a theme or plugin and the updates aren't reflecting on your website, ensure you've saved the modifications correctly. Clear your browser cache and website cache (if applicable) to ensure you're viewing the latest version. If the problem persists, check for any errors in your code or consult the theme/plugin documentation for troubleshooting steps.

## 6. How can I further customize my WordPress website beyond the available options?

**A:** For more extensive customization, consider learning CSS to modify styles and layouts. You can add custom CSS directly within your theme's stylesheet or use a plugin for easier management. For advanced functionality, exploring PHP and WordPress hooks can open up a world of possibilities.

## 7. What are some resources for staying updated on WordPress news and trends?

**A:** Follow reputable WordPress blogs, subscribe to newsletters, and participate in online communities to stay informed about the latest developments, security updates, and industry trends. Attending WordPress events or conferences can also provide valuable insights and networking opportunities.

**Remember**, these FAQs are just a glimpse into the vast landscape of possibilities within WordPress. Keep exploring, asking questions, and expanding your knowledge to unlock the full potential of this powerful platform.

# 17.6 Conclusion

Throughout this chapter, we've explored the essential skill of troubleshooting in the context of WordPress. By understanding how to identify problems, interpret error messages, and implement solutions, you've gained valuable tools to overcome challenges and maintain a healthy, functioning website.

Remember, troubleshooting is an ongoing process. As you continue your WordPress journey, you'll inevitably encounter new situations and issues. Embrace these as opportunities to expand your knowledge and refine your skills. The WordPress community is a vast and supportive network, offering a wealth of resources to guide you along the way.

In the next chapter, we'll delve deeper into the world of resources and further learning. You'll discover valuable tools, websites, communities, and educational materials to enhance your WordPress skills and take your website to the next level.

Keep exploring, keep learning, and most importantly, keep building. With dedication and the right resources, your WordPress website can become a powerful platform for sharing your ideas, connecting with your audience, and achieving your online goals.

***

# Chapter 18: Useful Resources and Further Learning

What will you learn:



## 18.1 Official WordPress Resources

The WordPress ecosystem thrives on its vibrant and supportive community, and the official WordPress resources serve as your gateway to this wealth of information, tools, and connections.

### 1. WordPress.org: The Central Hub

Your first stop should always be WordPress.org, the official website for everything WordPress. Here you can:

- **Download WordPress:** Get the latest version of WordPress software to start building your website.

- **Explore Themes and Plugins:** Discover thousands of free themes and plugins to enhance your website's functionality and design.

- **Read News and Updates:** Stay informed about the latest WordPress developments, security releases, and community events.

- **Access Documentation:** Find comprehensive documentation and tutorials covering all aspects of using and managing WordPress.

## 2. WordPress Codex: Your Comprehensive Manual

The WordPress Codex is an invaluable online manual meticulously curated by the community. It offers in-depth information on nearly every aspect of WordPress, including:

- **Installation and Configuration:** Guides on setting up your WordPress website and configuring essential settings.

- **Theme and Plugin Development:** Resources for developers looking to create custom themes and plugins.

- **API Reference:** Detailed documentation of WordPress functions, classes, and hooks for advanced customization.

- **Troubleshooting Guides:** Tips and solutions for common WordPress errors and issues.

## 3. WordPress Support Forums: Seeking Help from the Community

When you encounter a problem or have a specific question, the WordPress Support Forums are a go-to resource. Here you can:

- **Post Questions:** Seek assistance from experienced WordPress users and developers.

- **Search Existing Threads:** Find solutions to common issues that others have already discussed.

- **Contribute Your Knowledge:** Share your expertise and help others by answering questions and participating in discussions.

# 4. Make WordPress: Contributing to the Open-Source Project

WordPress is an open-source platform, meaning its code is publicly available and anyone can contribute to its development. The Make WordPress website provides a platform for getting involved:

- **Join a Team:** Explore various teams like Core, Design, Mobile, Accessibility, and more, each focusing on specific aspects of WordPress development.

- **Contribute Code or Translations:** If you have coding skills, you can contribute directly to the WordPress core software or translate WordPress into different languages.

- **Help with Documentation:** Assist in improving the WordPress Codex by writing and editing documentation.

By actively engaging with these official resources, you'll not only gain valuable knowledge and support but also become a part of the thriving WordPress community, contributing to the platform's growth and success.

# 18.2 Learning Platforms and Courses

While hands-on experience is invaluable, supplementing it with structured learning can significantly accelerate your WordPress journey. Thankfully, numerous platforms and courses cater to all skill levels, from absolute beginners to seasoned developers.

## Online Learning Platforms

- **Udemy:** Offers a vast library of WordPress courses covering various topics, from basic website creation to advanced development and design.

- **Coursera:** Provides access to university-level courses and specializations in WordPress development and related web technologies.

- **Skillshare:** Features a diverse range of creative WordPress courses, often focusing on design, content creation, and marketing aspects.

- **LinkedIn Learning:** Offers a curated selection of high-quality WordPress courses taught by industry experts, ideal for professional development.

## WordPress-Specific Training Websites

- **WP101:** Provides beginner-friendly video tutorials that cover WordPress basics in a clear and concise manner.

- **WP Apprentice:** Offers comprehensive courses and tutorials focusing on building and managing WordPress websites effectively.

- **Yoast Academy:** The team behind the popular Yoast SEO plugin provides in-depth courses on SEO, content creation, and website optimization.

## Local WordPress Meetups and Workshops

- **Meetup.com:** Discover local WordPress meetups in your area where you can connect with other users, attend workshops, and learn from experienced professionals.

- **WordPress Events Calendar:** Explore the official WordPress events calendar to find workshops, conferences, and meetups happening worldwide.

- **Community Colleges and Universities:** Many local educational institutions offer WordPress courses or workshops as part of their continuing education programs.

## Tips for Choosing a Learning Platform or Course

- **Identify your learning goals:** Determine your specific needs and skill level to choose the most relevant course.

- **Read reviews and ratings:** Get insights from other learners to gauge the quality and effectiveness of the course.

- **Consider the instructor's expertise:** Choose courses taught by experienced WordPress professionals with a proven track record.

- **Explore free options before committing to paid courses:** Many platforms offer introductory content or free trials to help you decide.

Continuous learning is key to mastering WordPress and unlocking its full potential. By exploring these learning platforms and courses, you can expand your knowledge, refine your skills, and stay ahead of the curve in the ever-evolving world of web development.

# 18.3 Freelancing Platforms to Get Hired

Finding work as a freelance WordPress developer can be exciting and rewarding. Luckily, there are numerous platforms available to connect you with clients seeking your skills. Here are platforms to explore:

## General Freelance Platforms

- **Upwork:** A popular platform with a vast pool of clients and projects, but also high competition.

- **Fiverr:** Known for its quick gigs and competitive pricing. Start with smaller projects and build your reputation.

- **Freelancer.com:** Similar to Upwork, with a wide range of projects and skill levels.

- **Guru:** Focuses on more experienced freelancers and offers various project management tools.

- **Toptal:** A premium platform with a rigorous screening process, attracting high-quality clients and projects.

- **PeoplePerHour:** Caters to hourly projects, making it ideal for smaller tasks and quick turnarounds.

## WordPress-Specific Freelance Platforms

- **Codeable.io:** Exclusively for WordPress developers, offering pre-vetted projects and competitive rates.

- **WP Hired:** Connects WordPress professionals with businesses seeking their expertise.

- **WP Jobs:** A job board specifically for WordPress-related roles, including freelance opportunities.

## Other Platforms to Consider

- **LinkedIn:** Leverage your network and actively engage in relevant groups to find opportunities.

- **Facebook Groups:** Join WordPress and web development groups to connect with potential clients.

- **Job Boards:** Explore niche job boards catering to web development and WordPress.

- **Your Own Website:** Showcase your portfolio and expertise to attract clients directly.

**Bonus .3:**

- **Local Networking Events:** Attend industry meetups and conferences to connect with potential clients and collaborators.

- **Content Marketing:** Share your knowledge through blog posts, tutorials, and social media to attract organic leads.

- **Word-of-Mouth Referrals:** Build strong relationships with past clients and colleagues to generate referrals.

## Tips for Success

- **Craft a strong profile:** Highlight your skills, experience, and portfolio to stand out from the competition.

- **Specialize in a niche:** Focusing on a specific area within WordPress can attract higher-paying clients.

- **Build your reputation:** Deliver high-quality work and excellent customer service to gain positive reviews and repeat clients.

- **Set competitive rates:** Research industry standards and adjust your pricing based on your experience and skills.

- **Be proactive:** Actively search for projects and reach out to potential clients.

By exploring these platforms and implementing these tips, you can increase your chances of landing freelance WordPress development projects and building a successful career. Remember, persistence and quality are key!

# 18.4 Client Collaboration Toolkit

Successful client collaboration hinges on clear communication and well-defined expectations. This toolkit equips you with essential documents and processes to foster strong partnerships and ensure project success. Remember, the samples provided in the annexure offer practical templates to adapt and utilize.

## 1. Proposals (Annexure A)

- **Purpose:** A proposal outlines your understanding of the client's needs, your proposed solution, and the value you bring. It's your chance to make a compelling case and secure the project.

- **Key elements:** Project overview, scope of work, timeline, deliverables, fees, your expertise and qualifications, and a call to action.

- **Tips:** Tailor your proposal to each client, highlighting relevant experience and showcasing your understanding of their specific challenges and goals.

## 2. Agreements (Annexure B)

- **Purpose:** A formal agreement, often a contract, protects both parties by outlining project specifics, terms, and conditions.

- **Key elements:** Scope of work, deliverables, timelines, payment terms, revisions, intellectual property rights, confidentiality clauses, and termination clauses.

- **Tips:** Ensure the agreement is comprehensive and clearly understood by both parties. Consider seeking legal advice for complex projects.

## 3. Project Report (Annexure C)

- **Purpose:** Regular progress reports keep clients informed, demonstrate your accountability, and build trust.

- **Key elements:** Project status updates, completed tasks, milestones achieved, upcoming deadlines, challenges encountered, and planned solutions.

- **Tips:** Choose a reporting format (written reports, presentations, or online dashboards) that aligns with client preferences and project needs.

## 4. Invoicing and Payment Processes (Annexure D)

- **Purpose:** Invoices document the services rendered and request payment, ensuring timely and accurate compensation.

- **Key elements:** Invoice number, date, client information, description of services, fees, payment terms, and payment methods.

- **Tips:** Use professional invoicing software or templates, clearly outline payment expectations, and follow up promptly on any outstanding invoices.

## Additional Tools for Collaboration

- **Project Management Software:** Platforms like Asana, Trello, or Basecamp facilitate task management, communication, and file sharing.

- **Communication Tools:** Utilize email, video conferencing, or instant messaging for regular updates and discussions.

- **Feedback Mechanisms:** Establish a system for gathering client feedback throughout the project to ensure satisfaction.

**Remember:** Effective documentation is crucial for building strong client relationships, preventing misunderstandings, and ensuring project success. Utilize this toolkit to streamline your processes and foster collaborative partnerships.

# 18.5 Community and Support

One of WordPress's greatest strengths is its vibrant and supportive community. Connecting with other users, sharing experiences, and seeking help when needed can significantly enhance your WordPress journey.

## WordPress Meetups

Local WordPress meetups offer invaluable opportunities to:

- **Connect with Fellow Users:** Meet other WordPress enthusiasts in your area, share experiences, and learn from each other's successes and challenges.

- **Attend Presentations and Workshops:** Gain insights from experienced speakers and participate in hands-on workshops to expand your skills.

- **Network and Collaborate:** Build valuable connections with other professionals and potential collaborators.

## Online Communities and Forums

Several online platforms provide spaces for WordPress users to connect and support each other:

- **WordPress Support Forums:** The official support forums remain a primary source for seeking help with specific issues, with dedicated sections for various topics.

- **Advanced WordPress Facebook Group:** This active Facebook group caters to more experienced users and developers, offering a platform for in-depth discussions and problem-solving.

- **WordPress Subreddit:** The WordPress subreddit is another vibrant community where users share news, tips, tutorials, and engage in lively discussions.

## Social Media Groups

- **Local WordPress Facebook Groups:** Many cities and regions have dedicated Facebook groups for local WordPress users to connect and share information.

- **Twitter:** Follow influential WordPress figures, developers, and organizations to stay updated on the latest news and trends.

- **LinkedIn Groups:** Join professional groups focused on WordPress to network with other professionals and discover job opportunities.

## Benefits of Engaging with the Community

- **Troubleshooting and Problem-Solving:** Get help with technical issues or challenges you encounter while using WordPress.

- **Learning and Inspiration:** Discover new tips, tricks, and best practices from experienced users and developers.

- **Staying Up-to-Date:** Keep yourself informed about the latest WordPress developments, trends, and security updates.

- **Networking and Collaboration:** Build valuable connections within the WordPress community and potentially find collaborators or clients.

**Remember**, the WordPress community is built on a spirit of sharing and mutual support. By actively participating in these communities, you'll not only gain valuable assistance but also contribute to the collective knowledge and growth of the WordPress ecosystem.

# 18.6 Development Resources

For those who want to delve deeper into WordPress development and customization, a wealth of resources exists to support your coding endeavors.

## Theme and Plugin Directories

- **WordPress Theme Directory:** Explore thousands of free themes with diverse designs and functionalities to find the perfect fit for your website.

- **WordPress Plugin Directory:** Discover a vast collection of free plugins that extend WordPress functionality, from SEO and security to e-commerce and social media integration.

## Code Reference and Documentation

- **WordPress Code Reference:** This comprehensive resource provides detailed information on WordPress functions, classes, hooks, and APIs, essential for understanding the inner workings of the platform.

- **PHP Manual:** Since WordPress is built on PHP, familiarizing yourself with the official PHP manual is crucial for understanding and writing custom code.

- **Developer Handbooks:** WordPress offers developer handbooks for specific topics like plugin development, theme development, REST API, and block editor development.

## Developer Tools and Plugins

- **Local Development Environments:** Tools like Local by Flywheel, XAMPP, or MAMP allow you to create local WordPress installations on your computer for testing and development without affecting your live website.

- **Code Editors and IDEs:** Choose from popular code editors like Visual Studio Code, Sublime Text, or Atom, or explore full-fledged Integrated Development Environments (IDEs) like PhpStorm for a more robust coding experience.

- **Version Control Systems:** Utilize Git, a popular version control system, for managing code changes, collaborating with other developers, and tracking revisions.

- **Debugging Tools:** Debugging plugins like Query Monitor or Debug Bar provide insights into your website's performance, database queries, and potential errors.

## Additional Resources

- **WP-CLI:** Learn to use the WordPress Command Line Interface (WP-CLI) for managing your WordPress installation, automating tasks, and performing bulk actions efficiently.

- **REST API Documentation:** Explore the WordPress REST API documentation to learn how to interact with your WordPress data programmatically and integrate with external applications.

- **Online Courses and Tutorials:** Numerous online resources offer in-depth tutorials and courses specifically focused on WordPress development, covering topics like theme creation, plugin development, and custom functionality.

**Remember,** WordPress development is an ongoing learning process. By leveraging these resources, experimenting with code, and seeking help from the community, you can continually expand your skills and build increasingly powerful and customized WordPress websites.

# 18.7 Inspiration and Design

Building a successful website involves more than just technical skills; it requires a keen eye for design and a touch of inspiration. Fortunately, the WordPress community offers a wealth of resources to fuel your creative vision and guide your design choices.

## Showcase Websites and Galleries

- **WordPress Showcase:** Explore the official WordPress showcase featuring a curated collection of stunning websites built with the platform, demonstrating diverse designs and functionalities across various industries.

- **Awwwards:** Discover award-winning websites recognized for their exceptional design, creativity, and user experience, often including projects built with WordPress.

- **Best Website Gallery:** Browse through curated collections of inspiring websites categorized by style, industry, and features.

## Design Blogs and Magazines

- **Smashing Magazine:** A leading online publication covering web design trends, best practices, user experience, and development tutorials, often featuring WordPress-specific content.

- **Webdesigner Depot:** Offers design inspiration, news, and resources for web designers and developers, including articles on WordPress themes and plugins.

- **Creative Bloq:** A hub for creative inspiration, with articles on web design, graphic design, and digital art, providing ideas to enhance your website's visual appeal.

## Free Stock Photo and Icon Resources

- **Unsplash:** Discover a vast collection of high-resolution, royalty-free images that you can use freely on your website.

- **Pexels:** Another excellent source for free stock photos and videos with a diverse range of categories and styles.

- **Flaticon:** Find a massive library of free icons in various styles and formats, perfect for enhancing your website's user interface.

## Additional Tips for Design Inspiration

- **Follow Design Leaders on Social Media:** Keep an eye on the work of renowned web designers and agencies to stay updated on current trends and best practices.

- **Analyze Your Favorite Websites:** Take note of design elements, layouts, and features that you find appealing on other websites and consider how you can adapt them to your own project.

- **Experiment with Different Themes and Plugins:** Explore the vast selection of WordPress themes and plugins to discover new design possibilities and functionalities.

- **Seek Feedback from Others:** Share your design ideas with friends, colleagues, or online communities to gather valuable feedback and perspectives.

**Remember**, design is an iterative process. Don't be afraid to experiment, explore different styles, and refine your vision until you achieve a website that not only functions flawlessly but also captivates your audience with its visual appeal and user experience.

# 18.8 Staying Updated

The world of WordPress is constantly evolving, with new features, security updates, and trends emerging regularly. Staying informed and adapting to these changes is crucial for maintaining a secure, efficient, and modern website.

## WordPress News and Blogs

- **WordPress News:** The official WordPress News section on WordPress.org provides announcements about the latest releases, security updates, and community events.

- **WPTavern:** A popular independent news website covering all things WordPress, including in-depth articles, interviews, and analysis of industry trends.

- **ManageWP Blog:** Offers valuable insights and tutorials on WordPress management, security, performance optimization, and business strategies.

## Official WordPress Social Media Channels

- **WordPress Twitter:** Follow @WordPress on Twitter for real-time updates, announcements, and engagement with the community.

- **WordPress Facebook Page:** Like the official WordPress Facebook page for news, articles, and discussions related to the platform.

- **WordPress YouTube Channel:** Subscribe to the WordPress

YouTube channel for video tutorials, event recordings, and developer updates.

## Industry Conferences and Events

- **WordCamp:** Attend WordCamps, locally organized conferences held worldwide, featuring presentations, workshops, and networking opportunities for WordPress users of all levels.

- **WooConf:** If you use WooCommerce for your online store, consider attending WooConf, the official WooCommerce conference, to learn about the latest e-commerce trends and best practices.

- **Other Industry Events:** Explore various industry conferences and events related to web design, development, and digital marketing to stay ahead of the curve and discover new tools and techniques.

## Additional Tips for Staying Updated

- **Subscribe to Newsletters:** Many WordPress-related websites and blogs offer email newsletters that deliver updates and insights directly to your inbox.

- **Join Online Communities:** Participating in active online forums, social media groups, and communities keeps you connected with the latest discussions and trends.

- **Follow Influencers:** Identify thought leaders and experts in the WordPress space and follow their blogs, social media channels, and publications.

- **Set Up Google Alerts:** Create Google Alerts for relevant keywords like "WordPress," "web design," or specific plugin names to receive notifications about new content and updates.

By actively engaging with these resources and maintaining a curious mindset, you'll ensure your WordPress knowledge remains current, allowing you to adapt to changes, implement best practices, and keep your website at the forefront of the digital landscape.

# 18.9 Conclusion: Your WordPress Journey Continues

As we reach the end of our exploration together, it's incredible to reflect on the journey we've taken through the world of WordPress. From understanding the fundamentals to building, customizing, and managing your website, you've acquired valuable skills and knowledge to confidently navigate this powerful platform.

The resources and tools explored in this chapter are your compass and map for continued learning and growth. The WordPress community, with its vast network of support and information, will always be there to guide you along the way. Remember, the learning never truly ends; embrace new challenges, explore emerging trends, and keep building upon the foundation you've established.

**This book has equipped you with the essentials**, but the possibilities with WordPress are limitless. With dedication and creativity, you can transform your website into a dynamic platform for sharing your ideas, connecting with your audience, and achieving your online aspirations.

Before you embark on the next phase of your WordPress journey, take a moment to review the glossary provided after this chapter. It offers a handy reference for key terms and concepts encountered throughout the book, solidifying your understanding and serving as a valuable resource for future reference.

***

# Glossary of Terms

A

- **Admin:** Short for administrator, this is the user role with the highest level of access and control over a WordPress website.

- **Apache:** A popular open-source web server software that is often used to host WordPress websites.

- **API:** Application Programming Interface. It allows different applications to communicate and share data with each other.

- **Attachment:** A file, such as an image, video, or document, that is uploaded to a WordPress website and linked to a post or page.

B

- **Backup:** A copy of your website's files and database that can be used to restore your site in case of data loss or technical issues.

- **Blog:** A type of website that features regularly updated content in the form of posts, typically displayed in reverse chronological order.

- **Block Editor (Gutenberg):** The default content editor in WordPress since version 5.0, allowing users to build pages and posts using a block-based system.

C

- **Caching:** The process of storing frequently accessed data in a temporary location to improve website loading speed.

- **Category:** A way to group related posts together, making it easier for users to navigate and find content on a website.

- **Child Theme:** A theme that inherits the functionality and styling of another theme (parent theme) while allowing for customizations without modifying the parent theme's code.

- **Content Management System (CMS):** A software application like WordPress that allows users to create, manage, and publish digital content without requiring extensive coding knowledge.

- **CSS (Cascading Style Sheets):** A coding language used to control the visual appearance and layout of a website.

**D**

- **Dashboard:** The main control panel of a WordPress website where users can manage content, customize settings, and access various features.

- **Database:** A structured collection of data that stores all the information related to a WordPress website, such as posts, pages, comments, and user data.

- **Domain Name:** The web address of your website, like "yourwebsite.com," that users type into their browser to access your site.

- **Draft:** A saved version of a post or page that has not yet been published.

**E**

- **Editor:** A user role with permissions to create, edit, publish, and manage posts and pages.

- **Excerpt:** A short summary of a post or page that is often displayed on archive pages or search results.

**F**

- **Featured Image:** An image that is chosen to represent a post or page, often displayed prominently on the website.

- **Footer:** The bottom section of a website that typically contains copyright information, contact details, and links to other pages.

- **Front-end:** The part of a website that visitors see and interact with.

**G**

- **Gravatar:** A Globally Recognized Avatar that is associated with a user's email address and displayed next to their comments on WordPress websites.

- **Gutenberg:** See "Block Editor."

**H**

- **Header:** The top section of a website that typically contains the website logo, navigation menu, and search bar.

- **HTML (HyperText Markup Language):** A coding language used to structure the content of a website.

- **Hosting:** A service that provides storage space and resources for your website's files and data, making it accessible on the internet.

- **HTTPS:** Hypertext Transfer Protocol Secure. A secure version of HTTP that encrypts data transmitted between a website and its visitors, providing additional security.

**I**

- **Image Optimization:** The process of reducing the file size of images without compromising quality to improve website loading speed.

**J**

- **JavaScript:** A scripting language that adds interactivity and dynamic features to websites.

**K**

- **Keyword:** A word or phrase that describes the content of a website or post, used in SEO to improve search engine rankings.

**L**

- **Link:** A connection between two web pages or websites, allowing users to navigate between them.

- **Login:** The process of entering your username and password to access the WordPress dashboard.

## M

- **Media Library:** A central location in WordPress where all uploaded media files, such as images and videos, are stored and managed.

- **Menu:** A navigation element that provides links to different pages or sections of a website.

- **Meta Description:** A brief summary of a web page that appears in search engine results, providing information about the page's content.

- **Mobile Responsive:** A website design that adapts to different screen sizes and devices, providing an optimal viewing experience for users on desktops, tablets, and smartphones.

## N

- **Navigation Menu:** A list of links that helps users navigate through the different pages and sections of a website.

## P

- **Page:** A static piece of content on a WordPress website, such as an About page, Contact page, or landing page.

- **Permalink:** The permanent URL of a specific post or page on a WordPress website.

- **PHP:** The scripting language that powers WordPress, used to process code and interact with the database.

- **Plugin:** A software add-on that extends the functionality of a WordPress website, adding new features and capabilities.

- **Post:** A type of content on a WordPress website that is typically displayed in reverse chronological order and can be categorized or tagged.

**R**

- **Responsive Design:** A web design approach that ensures a website adapts and displays optimally on different screen sizes and devices.

- **Revisions:** A feature in WordPress that automatically saves different versions of posts and pages as you edit them, allowing you to revert to previous versions if needed.

- **Role:** A level of access and permissions assigned to users on a WordPress website, such as Administrator, Editor, Author, or Subscriber.

- **RSS Feed:** A standardized format for distributing website content, allowing users to subscribe and receive updates through RSS readers.

**S**

- **SEO (Search Engine Optimization):** The practice of optimizing a website to improve its ranking in search engine results pages (SERPs).

- **Shortcode:** A small piece of code that allows you to embed dynamic content or functionality within posts or pages.

- **Sidebar:** A vertical column on a website that typically contains widgets, navigation links, or other information.

- **Slider:** A slideshow of images or content that is often displayed prominently on a website's homepage.

- **Slug:** The part of a URL that identifies a specific page or post, typically based on the title.

- **Social Media Integration:** The use of plugins or features that allow you to connect your website with social media platforms for sharing content and engaging with your audience.

**T**

- **Tag:** A keyword or label that is assigned to a post to categorize it and make it easier to find.

- **Theme:** A collection of files that determine the design and layout of a WordPress website.

- **Thumbnail:** A smaller version of an image that is used as a preview.

**U**

- **URL (Uniform Resource Locator):** The web address of a specific page or file on the internet.

- **User:** An individual who has an account on a WordPress website and can interact with the site based on their assigned role and permissions.

**W**

- **Widget:** A small block of content or functionality that can be added to a website's sidebar, footer, or other designated areas.

- **WordPress.com:** A hosted platform that allows you to create a WordPress website without the need for self-hosting.

- **WordPress.org:** The open-source platform where you can download the WordPress software and host your website on your own server.

**X**

- **XML (Extensible Markup Language):** A markup language that is used to structure and organize data for various applications, including RSS feeds.

**Z**

- **Zip File:** A compressed file format that is often used to package and distribute WordPress themes and plugins

***

# Conclusion

# Summary and Final Thoughts

Congratulations! You've reached the end of your WordPress journey with "WordPress for Everyone: Build Websites without Coding." By now, you should have a solid understanding of how to navigate the WordPress dashboard, build pages and posts, customize your website's appearance, and even implement basic SEO practices. You've equipped yourself with the tools and knowledge to create a website that reflects your unique vision, all without writing a single line of code.

## Summary: A Look Back at Your Journey

Let's take a moment to recap the key milestones of your WordPress adventure:

- **Setting Up Your Website:** You learned how to choose a hosting provider, register a domain name, and install WordPress, laying the foundation for your online presence.

- **Mastering the Dashboard:** We delved into the WordPress dashboard, familiarizing ourselves with its layout and the purpose of each section.

- **Themes and Customization:** We explored the world of themes, learning how to select, install, and customize them to achieve your desired website aesthetic.

- **Plugins and Functionality:** You learned how plugins extend the functionality of your website, adding features like contact forms, SEO optimization, and social media integration.

- **SEO Basics:** We touched upon the importance of SEO and explored basic techniques to improve your website's visibility in search engine results.

## Final Thoughts: Your Website, Your Journey

Building a website with WordPress is an ongoing process. As you become more comfortable with the platform, you'll discover new ways to enhance your site and achieve your online goals. Remember, there are countless resources available to support you on your journey, including the official WordPress documentation, online tutorials, and a vibrant community of WordPress users and developers.

Here are a few final thoughts to keep in mind:

- **Experiment and explore:** Don't be afraid to try new things and experiment with different features and plugins.

- **Content is king:** Focus on creating high-quality content that is relevant and engaging for your target audience.

- **Keep learning:** The world of WordPress is constantly evolving, so stay updated with the latest trends and technologies.

- **Join the community:** Connect with other WordPress users and developers to share knowledge, seek support, and learn from each other.

**Remember,** your website is a reflection of you and your unique voice. Embrace the journey, keep learning, and enjoy the process of creating something special in the online world.

*** 

# Annexure

# Proposal

**Client:**

**Date:**

## 1. Introduction

- Briefly introduce yourself and your company (if applicable).
- Highlight your experience and expertise in WordPress development.
- Briefly state your understanding of the client's needs and goals.

## 2. Project Overview

- **Project Name:**
- **Project Goals:**
- **Target Audience:**
- **Website Type:**

## 3. Scope of Work

- **Website Design:**
  - Theme development or customization
  - Number of pages/sections
  - Responsive design implementation
  - Branding and visual identity
- **Website Functionality:**
  - E-commerce functionality (if applicable)
  - Plugin integration
  - Custom features and functionalities
  - Content Management System (CMS) training
- **Content Migration (if applicable):**
  - Transferring content from an existing website
  - Content formatting and optimization

## 4. Timeline

- **Project Start Date:**
- **Estimated Completion Date:**
- **Key Milestones:** [List major project phases and their estimated deadlines]

## 5. Deliverables

List all final deliverables, including:

- Developed WordPress website
- Design files (if applicable)
- Documentation and user manuals (if applicable)
- Training materials (if applicable)

## 6. Fees and Payment Terms

- **Project Fee:**
- **Payment Schedule:**
- **Payment Methods:**

## 7. Your Qualifications

- Briefly showcase your relevant skills and experience.
- Highlight past projects and successes.
- Mention any relevant certifications or awards.

## 8. Call to Action

- Clearly state the next steps for moving forward.
- Express your enthusiasm for the project and your commitment to the client's success.

## 9. Annexure (Optional):

- Include any additional supporting documents, such as:
  - Portfolio of past work
  - Client testimonials
  - Detailed project breakdown
  - Team member bios

*****Please note: This is a general template and should be customized to fit the specific needs of each project and client.**

***

# Agreement

This Agreement is made and entered into as of [DATE] by and between [CLIENT NAME], with a principal place of business at [CLIENT ADDRESS] ("Client") and [YOUR NAME/COMPANY NAME], with a principal place of business at [YOUR ADDRESS] ("Developer").

WHEREAS, Client desires to engage Developer to provide WordPress development services, and Developer desires to provide such services;

NOW, THEREFORE, in consideration of the mutual covenants contained herein, the parties agree as follows:

## 1. Services

Developer agrees to perform the following services ("Services"):

[Detailed description of the services, including website development, design, theme customization, plugin integration, etc.]

[Specify any limitations or exclusions]

## 2. Deliverables

Developer shall deliver the following to Client upon completion of the Services ("Deliverables"):

[List all final deliverables, such as the developed WordPress website, design files, documentation, training materials, etc.]

## 3. Timeline

- Project Start Date: [Date]
- Estimated Completion Date: [Date]
- Key Milestones: [List major project phases and their estimated deadlines]

## 4. Fees and Payment

- Project Fee: [Total project cost]
- Payment Schedule: [Outline the payment schedule, e.g., upfront payment, milestones, or upon completion]
- Payment Methods: [Specify accepted payment methods]

- Late Payment: [Outline any late payment fees or penalties]

## 5. Client Responsibilities

Client agrees to:

- Provide all necessary content and materials in a timely manner.
- Respond promptly to Developer's requests for information or feedback.
- Cooperate with Developer in all phases of the project.

## 6. Intellectual Property Rights

- [Specify ownership of intellectual property rights for the developed website, theme, plugins, and other materials]
- [Address licensing agreements for any third-party software or resources used]

## 7. Confidentiality

Both parties agree to maintain the confidentiality of any sensitive information disclosed during the course of the project.

## 8. Termination

This Agreement may be terminated by either party for breach of contract or upon [NUMBER] days' written notice.

## 9. Warranty and Limitation of Liability

Developer warrants that the Services will be performed in a professional and workmanlike manner.

[Specify any limitations of liability or disclaimers]

## 10. Independent Contractor

Developer is an independent contractor and not an employee of Client.

## 11. Governing Law

This Agreement shall be governed by and construed in accordance with the laws of the State of [COUNTRY/STATE].

## 12. Entire Agreement

This Agreement constitutes the entire agreement between the parties and supersedes all prior or contemporaneous communications, representations, or agreements, whether oral or written.

IN WITNESS WHEREOF, the parties have executed this Agreement as of the date first written above.

**Client:**

[Signature]

[Printed Name]

**Developer:**

[Signature]

[Printed Name]

***Please note: This is a sample agreement and should be reviewed and modified by a legal professional to fit the specific needs of your project and comply with local laws and regulations.**

***

# Project Report

**Project Name:** [Project Name]
**Client:** [Client Name]
**Reporting Period**: [Date] to [Date]

## 1. Project Overview
- Briefly summarize the project's goals and objectives.
- State the current phase of the project.

## 2. Progress Summary
- **Completed Tasks:**
  - List all tasks completed during the reporting period.
  - Include specific details about each completed task.
- **Milestones Achieved:**
  - Highlight any major milestones reached during this period.
- **Challenges Encountered:**
  - Describe any obstacles or challenges faced during the period.
  - Explain how these challenges were addressed or mitigated.

## 3. Upcoming Tasks and Deadlines
- Outline the key tasks planned for the next reporting period.
- Specify deadlines for each upcoming task.
- Mention any potential challenges or dependencies that may impact progress.

## 4. Budget and Timeline Status
- Briefly summarize the project's current budget status.
- Indicate if the project is on track, ahead of schedule, or behind schedule.
- Explain any deviations from the original timeline or budget.

## 5. Communication and Collaboration
- Summarize key communication and collaboration activities during the period.
- Mention any meetings, discussions, or decisions made.
- Highlight any outstanding issues requiring client feedback or input.

## 6. Next Steps

- Clearly outline the next steps for the project.
- Specify any actions required from the client.
- Reiterate upcoming deadlines and milestones.

**7. Appendix (Optional)**
Include any supporting documents or visuals, such as:
- Screenshots of progress
- Design mockups
- Updated project timeline
- Meeting minutes

*****Please note: This is a sample report and should be customized to fit the specific details of your project and client preferences.**

**Additional Tips:**

- **Clarity and Conciseness:** Keep the report focused and easy to understand, avoiding technical jargon.
- **Visuals:** Use graphs, charts, or screenshots to illustrate progress and key data points.
- **Professionalism:** Maintain a professional tone and format throughout the report.
- **Consistency:** Use a consistent reporting format and schedule to establish clear expectations.

By providing regular project reports, you demonstrate transparency, accountability, and commitment to client satisfaction.

***

# Invoice

[Your Name/Company Name]
[Your Address]
[Your Phone Number]
[Your Email Address]

**Invoice Number:** [Unique Invoice Number]
**Invoice Date:** [Date]
**Bill To:**[Client Name][Client Address]
**Project:** [Project Name]

| Sr. No. | Description | Rate | Quantity | Amount |
|---|---|---|---|---|
| 1 | Website Development | | | |
| 2 | Migration | | | |
| 3 | | | | |
| | | | Subtotal | |
| | | | Tax | |
| | | | **Total** | |

**Payment Terms:** [Payment terms, e.g., Net 30 days]
**Payment Methods:** [Accepted payment methods, e.g., Bank transfer, PayPal]

**Notes:**

[Include any additional notes or information]
[Thank the client for their business]

*****Please note: This is a sample invoice and should be customized to fit your specific branding, services, and payment terms.**

**Additional Tips:**

- **Professionalism:** Use a clean and professional layout.
- **Clarity:** Clearly itemize all services and fees.
- **Accuracy:** Double-check all calculations to ensure accuracy.
- **Branding:** Incorporate your logo and brand colors.
- **Payment Options:** Offer multiple payment methods for client convenience.
- **Invoicing Software:** Consider using invoicing software for automated invoice generation and tracking.

By providing clear and professional invoices, you ensure smooth and timely payments while maintaining a positive client relationship.

***